CULTURES OF THE WORLD

Czech Republic

Efstathia Sioras and Michael Spilling

Marshall Cavendish Benchmark
New York

PICTURE CREDITS

Cover: © Bill Bachmann/Danita Delimont

Adam Woolfit/ Corbis: 102 • Audrius Tomonis: 135 • Christer Fredriksson/ Lonely Planet Images: 11 • David Neff/ AFP/ Getty Images: 31 • epa/Corbis: 107 • Eye Ubiquitous/Hutchison NMR: 50, 60, 64, 75, 94, 96, 106, 115 • Focus Team—Italy: 39, 70 • Gavin Hellier/Robert Harding World Imagery/ Corbis: 18 • George McCarthy/Corbis: 14 • HBL Network Photo Agency: 19 • Hutchison: 77, 113 • Jarmila Kovarikova/Isifa/Getty Images: 42• Jonathan Smith/ Lonely Planet Images: 15, 20, 124 • Libor Fojtik/Isifa/ Getty Images: 33 • Michal Cizek/AFP/Getty Images: 30, 38, 112 • North Wind Pictures Archives: 25 • Petr Josek/ alttype/Reuters: 10, 41 • photolibrary: 1, 56, 57, 58, 61, 66, 69, 71, 72, 76, 78, 80, 82, 87, 88, 90, 92, 95, 97, 98, 99, 100, 104, 108, 110, 111, 118, 119, 125, 126, 127, 128, 129, 130, 131 • Radim Beznoska/Isifa/Getty Images: 46 • Richard Nebesky/ Lonely Planet Images: 2, 5, 6, 7, 8, 9, 17, 23, 40, 51, 52, 103, 116, 122 • Sean Gallup/Getty Images: 45 • Stephen Saks/ Lonely Planet Images: 34 • Tan Lee Chung: 12, 16 • Tom Stoddart/ Getty Images: 54 • Tomas Hudcovic/ Isifa/Getty Images: 29 • Topham Picturepoint: 27, 28 • Travel Ink: 49 • Trip Photographic Library: 13, 48, 74, 84, 86 • Yuri Kadobnov/ AFP/ Getty Images: 36

PRECEDING PAGE

Two traditionally dressed girls in Prague.

Publisher (U.S.): Michelle Bisson
Editors: Deborah Grahame, Stephanie Pee
Copyreader: Daphne Hougham
Designers: Nancy Sabato, Rachel Chen
Cover picture researcher: Connie Gardner
Picture researcher: Thomas Khoo

Marshall Cavendish Benchmark
99 White Plains Road
Tarrytown, NY 10591
Website: www.marshallcavendish.us

Originated and designed by Marshall Cavendish International (Asia) Private Limited
A member of Times Publishing Limited

All Internet sites were correct and accurate at the time of printing. All monetary figures in this publication are in U.S. dollars.

Library of Congress Cataloging-in-Publication Data
Sioras, Efstathia.
Czech Republic / by Efstathia Sioras and Michael Spilling.
p. cm. -- (Cultures of the world)
Includes bibliographical references and index.
ISBN 978-0-7614-4476-3
1. Czech Republic--Juvenile literature. I. Spilling, Michael. II. Title.
DB2065.S56 2010
943.71—dc22 2009003185

Printed in China
7 6 5 4 3 2 1

CONTENTS

INTRODUCTION

THE CZECH REPUBLIC is a new country that was formed after the breakup of Czechoslovakia. It officially became an independent country on January 1, 1993. Czechia, the new republic's official short name, joined the North Atlantic Treaty Organization (NATO) in 1999 and the European Union (EU) in 2004.

Located in the center of Europe, the land and people that form the Czech Republic have contributed to a diverse and rich history spanning more than a thousand years. Although freedom of expression was curtailed during its communist era, the country has produced many world-famous writers, poets, musicians, and composers.

The Czech countryside is dominated by forests, hills, and mountains. Many of its cities and towns have well-preserved historical building sites ranging from medieval squares to Baroque churches.

Although the Czech people have often been subjected to foreign rule, they maintain a strong sense of cultural identity. In spite of the many changes it has experienced, the Czech Republic today is a thriving free nation with a strong economy.

GEOGRAPHY

Panská Rock formation near Kamenický Senov in the Lusetian Mountains.

CHAPTER 1

The Czech Republic is a landlocked country located in the heart of Europe. Its landscape is varied, ranging from flatlands in Bohemia to hilly regions in Moravia. The Czech Republic has three primary rivers, the Elbe, Oder, and Morava. All of the water in the Czech Republic drains into different seas: the North Sea, the Baltic Sea and the Black Sea.

THE CZECH REPUBLIC, a landlocked country, shares its borders with Austria (to the south), Germany (to the north and west), Poland (to the north), and the Republic of Slovakia (to the east and southeast). Slovakia and the Czech Republic together constituted Czechoslovakia until 1992. It is slightly smaller than the American state of South Carolina.

The country's geography is neatly divided between agricultural land and forests. Continuous forest belts border the mountains, while the lowlands have traditionally been developed for agricultural uses. Although large areas of original forest have been cleared for cultivation and for timber, thick woodlands remain a dominant feature of the Czech landscape.

Farmland in Zlinsky.

The snow-covered Elbe, or Labe River.

The republic's scenery varies dramatically from limestone caves and natural springs to beautiful mountain ranges and numerous rivers. Cities and towns are well distributed throughout the land.

BOHEMIA TO THE WEST

The Czech Republic consists of two major regions: Bohemia to the west and Moravia to the east. Their landscapes differ; Bohemia is essentially a 1,640 foot (500 m) high plateau surrounded by low mountains, while Moravia, particularly east Moravia, is hilly.

It is estimated that one-third of forest trees in the Czech Republic have been damaged by air pollution, acid rain, and parasites.

Bohemia is drained by the Elbe River (also called the Labe River), which provides access to the North Sea. Its tributary, the Vltava River (also called the Moldau River), at 270 miles (435 km), is the longest river in the Czech Republic. The region's chief towns are Prague, Plzeň, and České Budějovice.

Providing natural frontiers for Bohemia are the Šumava Mountains to the southwest, the Ore Mountains to the northwest (forming the border

An aerial view of the North Bohemia countryside in the Labe Sandstone region.

with Germany), the Riesengebirge (also called the Krkonoše or Giant) Mountains along the Polish border to the northeast, and the Bohemian-Moravian Highlands that divide Bohemia and Moravia. Mount Sněžka (5,256 feet/1,602 m) is the highest mountain in the republic and is part of the Giant Mountain range.

Bohemia is subdivided into five areas: North, South, East, West, and Central Bohemia. The topography of South Bohemia is unusual. Since the 16th century, the land around the city of České Budějovice has been gradually sculpted into a network of hundreds of linked fishponds and artificial lakes. Today they are used to farm-raise carp, a popular Christmas fish dish in Bohemia.

The republic's largest artificial lake is also located in the south, near Třeboň: Lake Rožmberk was created in 1590 and covers about 1,235 acres (500 ha). The republic's other large body of water is the lake behind Lipno Dam, near the Austrian border.

North Bohemia has long been the most highly industrialized region of the Czech Republic. Because it is the site of extensive coal and iron ore mining, North Bohemia has suffered severe air pollution. Over the last decade, however, there has been an enormous effort to improve the whole environment and the quality of the region's air. Today, people in parts of North Bohemia breathe a cleaner air and enjoy a greener landscape than in the recent past.

MORAVIA TO THE EAST

A stalactite (Greek *stalaktites*, from the word for "drip" and meaning "that which drips") is a type of speleothem (secondary mineral) that hangs from the ceilings or walls of limestone caves. It is sometimes referred to as drip-stone. A stalagmite (from the Greek *stalagma*, "drop" or "drip") is a type of speleothem that rises from the floor of a limestone cave due to the dripping of mineralized solutions, mainly the drop-by-drop piling up of calcium carbonate.

Essentially lowland, Moravia is also surrounded by mountains: to the west the Bohemian-Moravian Highlands, to the east the White Carpathian and the Javorníky mountains, and to the north the Jeseníky Mountains. Moravia's chief cities are Ostrava and Brno. Moravia is divided into North and South Moravia. In northeast Moravia there is also a historical region named Silesia. Silesia was a Polish province that was passed to Bohemia in 1335 and taken by Prussia in 1742. Most of Silesia was returned to Poland in 1945; the rest forms part of Germany and the Czech Republic. The two main rivers in this region are the Morava River, which flows south to the Danube and eventually drains into the Black Sea, and the Oder (also called Odra) River, which swings around the eastern end of the Sudeten Range into Poland and drains into the Baltic Sea. The Oder River caused extensive flooding in mid-1997: A third

A man reinforcing Morava River dikes in 2004 in anticipation of oncoming floodwaters.

of the republic was flooded for 10 days. Over 40 people died, 2,500 were injured, and 10,000 became homeless. Because of the devastation of the agricultural land, the republic had to import 440,800 tons (400,000 metric tonnes) of grain to prevent a food shortage.

In the southwest, just north of the city of Brno, lies the wooded highland area called the Moravian Karst, where limestone hills have been carved into canyons and hundreds of caves. Over millions of years, mildly acidic rainwater has seeped through the limestone rock, slowly dissolving sections of it. This has resulted in cave formations filled with colorful stalactites and stalagmites.

The Vltava Moldau River is one of the many beloved rivers that flow through the Czech Republic.

South Moravia is renowned for its wineries, which export some excellent wines. This area also produces some fiery plum and apricot brandies, the favorite distilled alcoholic beverages of the Czechs.

RIVERS

There are three principal river systems in the Czech Republic: the Elbe, Oder, and Morava rivers and their tributaries. The country's rivers flow to three different seas: those in southern Moravia flow to the Danube and onward to the Black Sea, the Elbe flows to the North Sea, and the Oder to the Baltic Sea. The journeys these rivers make are long: the Black Sea is 466 miles (750 km) to the southeast, the North Sea is 329 miles (530 km) to the northwest, and the Baltic Sea is 217 miles (350 km) to the north.

A VARIABLE CLIMATE

The Czech Republic has a humid continental climate. There are four distinct seasons, including hot, wet summers and cold, drier winters.

Fall coloring of leaves brightens the landscape near Cesky Krumlove.

Temperature and rainfall fluctuate greatly because of variable air pressure—the republic is known for its changeable weather.

In Moravia there is a wide variation in temperature between winter and summer, and day and night, whereas Bohemia receives the moderating influence of an oceanic climate, so day and night temperatures do not vary much. More rain and more frequent cloudy weather are found in Bohemia than in Moravia.

Average summer temperatures range between 70°F and 80°F (21°C and 27°C). Lowland temperatures often rise above 86°F (30°C). July is the hottest month of the year. In summer it rains, on average, every other day, with hot spells usually broken by heavy thunderstorms. In the highlands temperatures are generally cooler, as they fall with increasing elevation; mountain dwellers often experience near-freezing conditions.

Winter temperatures in the Czech Republic average between 25°F and 28°F (−4°C and −2°C), with January being the coldest month. Temperatures can drop to 5°F (−15°C) in the lowlands, and it can be bitterly cold in the highlands surrounding the Bohemian plateau, where Prague is situated.

Snow and fog are common in the lowlands, with 40 to 100 days of snow in the winter. Typically, there are 130 days of snow in the mountains. The Czech Republic does not have a really dry season. The winter months are slightly drier, with rainfall occurring one day in every three, averaging 20 to 30 inches (50 to 76 cm) annually in the lowlands and 32 inches (81 cm) or more in the highlands.

The Czech Republic is located in the main European watershed (the line that divides the drainage basins of the major rivers of Germany). Many central European rivers originate there. The country's main freshwater source is the precipitation that forms rivers. Rivers are at their highest in the spring and at their lowest in summer. There are also a few freshwater lakes. Most lakes, such as those in southern Bohemia, are man-made and provide a reliable source of fish for local consumption.

FLORA AND FAUNA

The Czech landscape, from agricultural lowlands to steppes and mountain ranges, supports a wide range of vegetation. Despite several hundred years of clear-cutting for cultivation and decades of unregulated industrial development, one-third of the republic is still covered by forest. Deciduous trees such as oaks are found in the lower regions of Moravia. Spruce is common in the lower mountain areas, and beech at higher elevations. Together, beech and spruce forests cover the mountains in the country. Dwarf pine is seen near the tree line. Above the tree line (approximately 4,595 feet/1,400 m) only grasses, shrubs, and lichens thrive.

The Green Roof of Europe–trees in the Bohemian Forest in West Moravia.

The Czech Republic is rich in fauna. Agricultural practices have allowed certain species, such as hamsters, to sustain large populations. Introduced species have spread rapidly, for example, muskrat, pheasant, and trout. A large variety of wildlife inhabits lower areas of the mountains: bears (almost extinct now), wolves, lynx, foxes, wildcats, marmots, otters, marten, deer, and mink. The chamois, a small mountain antelope hunted for its beautiful coat, came dangerously close to extinction. It is now protected, and its numbers are increasing.

A male capercaillie displays his plummage.

Hunted wildlife common to the woodlands and marshes are hares, rabbits, hamsters, gophers, partridge, pheasant, ducks, and wild geese. Protected species include the large birds: golden eagles, vultures, ospreys, storks, bustards, eagle-owls, and capercaillie (large grouse).

The country's national parks include the Bohemian Forest and the Krkonoše Mountains. The Bohemian Forest is part of an ecotourism project shared by the Czech Republic, Austria, and the state of Bavaria in Germany. Known as the Green Roof of Europe, this beautiful area attracts tourists who come to enjoy its wildlife as well as outdoor activities such as hiking and cycling.

CITIES

Over hundreds of years, towns in the region of the Czech Republic developed amid a dense network of settlements, many just a few miles from each other. Today, such towns number approximately 15,300. Growth

A closeup of the intricate astronomical clockface on Prague's Old Town Hall.

was irregular and typically has resulted in villages of fewer than 5,000 inhabitants. These small towns, classified as rural settlements, make up 98 percent of all communities in the Czech Republic. With a total population of approximately 10.22 million, there are 343.2 persons per square mile (132.5 persons per square km). In comparison, the average density in the United States is about 84.4 persons per square mile (32.6 persons per square km). The greatest density is to be found in industrial areas such as North Bohemia, while the lowest density is along the border in South Bohemia.

Prior to the industrial revolution, Czechs cultivated the land they lived on. With industrialization, urban areas burgeoned and changed the Czechs' relationship with the land. This has generally resulted in environmental degradation, overcrowding, and a decline in the quality of life.

Because of this deterioration in urban areas, many Czechs purchase vacation homes in the less affected countryside. Farms and old village houses are bought and renovated. This trend has saved much rural architecture that otherwise would have fallen to ruins. Regrettably, the construction of new second homes has damaged valuable agricultural land in some areas.

The government has responded to the concerns of Czechs over the adverse environmental effects of unregulated industrial development and urban sprawl. It curtailed extensive growth of towns and villages at the expense of agricultural land and forests. It has also encouraged greater density in existing urban areas and the redevelopment of derelict inner-city areas. The introduction of the 1996 Czech Republic Forest Act into Czech legislation and the formation of Natura 2000 have helped to improve and protect the forests and areas of natural beauty.

PRAGUE A legend about Prague tells of a princess of a Slav group known as the Czechs, so named after the leader of the group. The girl's name was Libuše. She stood upon a high rock above the river Vltava and uttered the following prophecy: "I see a city whose splendor shall reach the stars." She instructed her people to build a castle on the spot where a man was seen

View of the Old Town Square in Prague, heart of Czech history since the ninth century.

building the threshold of a house. Since threshold is *prah* in Czech, she asked them to name the castle Praha. Her people carried out her wishes. Two hundred years later, her prophecy came true: the city of Prague became the seat of the Přemysl dynasty.

Prague is at the geographical middle of Central Bohemia. It has flourished at the heart of Czech history since the Great Bohemian Empire in the ninth century. The republic's longest river, the Vltava, flows through the city. Affectionately named "the city of 100 spires," Prague displays Romanesque, Gothic, Renaissance, Baroque, and Art Nouveau styles of architecture. Several bridges link the west and east banks of the Vltava, but its landmark bridge is the stone Charles Bridge, begun in 1357 and lined with sculptures, the earliest placed in 1683, the most recent in 1928.

Prague is organized into several historical districts. On the west bank is the castle district of Hradčany with its 1,100-year-old castle and the magnificent

Construction of the Charles Bridge, one of Prague's most famous landmarks, began in 1357.

14th century Saint Vitus Cathedral. To its south is the 13th century Lesser Quarter, where the workers lived. On the east bank is the Old Town with its central enormous Old Town Square. The New Town, built in the 14th century, curves around the Old Town and Wenceslas Square, the site of many political events.

Prague is one of Europe's most popular tourist destinations. With a population of around 1.21 million, it is home to a large artistic community spanning the visual and literary arts as well as the music scene.

BRNO This city has a population of around 370,000 and is the second largest city in the Czech Republic. Dating from the Great Moravian Empire, Brno became the capital of Moravia in the 14th century. For many centuries the city remained devoutly Catholic in a mainly Protestant country, eventually becoming Protestant in the late 1500s. During the Austro-Hungarian Empire, it developed a strong textile industry. In 1919 a university was founded in the city. Today Brno is known for the many colorful trade fairs held at the exhibition grounds, the annual motorcycle grand prix, and its international music festival.

An aerial view of the city of Brno with the famous twin spires of Saint Peter's Cathedral.

OLOMOUC Legend has it that Julius Caesar founded Olomouc. In the 11th century, after the unification of Bohemia and Moravia, Olomouc became a major seat of administrative power. It was the capital of Moravia for several centuries in the Middle Ages. Today it is home to 100,000 inhabitants and is the fifth largest city in the Czech Republic. The town sits on a gentle bend of the Morava River. Olomouc, a university town, displays historical architecture second only to Prague. The town has Baroque-style fountains with classical themes: Hercules, Mercury, Neptune, Jupiter, and imperial founder Caesar. Cobbled streets wind through squares built in the Renaissance, Baroque, and Empire styles.

The spa town of Karlovy Vary is also known as Carlsbad.

KARLOVY VARY Situated in the protected Slavkov Forest in the northwest, 1,476 feet (450 m) above sea level, Karlovy Vary (known as Carlsbad in English) is the oldest of the Bohemian spa towns. Its 12 springs are located in or near colonnaded buildings. Folklore claims that King Charles IV was hunting in the nearby woods when a rising jet of hot water scalded his dog. Mineral springs are believed to possess medicinal properties; so Charles IV built a hunting lodge near the biggest spring and gave the town his name, Carlsbad (Charles's spa). The health-driven town developed a vibrant cultural life, too. The great poet Goethe visited often, and so did composers Bach, Beethoven, Brahms, Wagner, and Liszt. The annual Dvořák Music Festival attracts many visitors in September, and modern art movements such as Art Nouveau have been centered there. Another significant festival that takes place every summer is the Karlovy Vary International Film Festival. In 2008 the festival celebrated its 43rd year.

HISTORY

Saint Nicholas Church in Prague's Old Town Square. It was completed in 1735.

CHAPTER 2

THE HISTORY OF THE CZECH LANDS and people is over 1,000 years old and is replete with conquests and foreign rule. Only since January 1, 1993, though, have Czechs enjoyed independent statehood. The path that took them there is a complex and fascinating one.

EARLY TRACES OF CIVILIZATION

Humans inhabited the Czech lands more than 600,000 years ago. Evidence exists of established farming communities in the lowlands from approximately 4000 B.C. The Celts and Germans were the first peoples to inhabit the area.

THE GREAT MORAVIAN EMPIRE

By A.D. 600 the Slavic ancestors of today's Czechs had settled in the area, calling themselves Moravians, after the Morava River. They united under Mojmír I, who ruled from 818 to 846. Archaeological remains have been discovered in Moravia dating to this period. His Great Moravian Empire included modern-day western Slovakia, Bohemia, Silesia, parts of eastern Germany, southeastern Poland, and northern Hungary.

During the reign of the second ruler of the Moravian Empire, Rostislav, who is also referred to as Rastislav (846—870), the written Slavic language came into existence. At Rostislav's request, the Byzantine

The history of the Czech Republic is an extensive and colorful one. During World War II it was not spared the advances of its Nazi neighbor, Germany. Czech Republic was subsequently governed under communist rule, but oppressive censorship and harsh economic conditions led to a growing dissatisfaction with communism. This culminated in the Velvet Revolution and finally, to the Velvet Divorce.

SAINT WENCESLAS

Wenceslas I (c. 903—935), duke of Bohemia, was one of the early Přemysl rulers. Václav, as he was named, succeeded his father, chief of the Czech group occupying the western part of Central Bohemia, in 921; but his mother, Drahomíra, ruled as regent until 924 or 925. During his reign Wenceslas extended his dominion in Bohemia.

Czechs consider him the founder of the Czech state, although the Slavic peoples did not become a cohesive force until after his death. Good King Wenceslas was an educated man, and legends stress his Christian values. His submission to German king Henry I, the Fowler, may be the reason behind his brother Boleslav's conspiracy to murder him in 935. His murder was viewed as martyrdom, and by the beginning of the 11th century he had attained sainthood. Saint Wenceslas is today the patron saint of Bohemia.

Czech legend proclaims that Saint Wenceslas lies sleeping, along with other Czech knights, under Blaník Mountain in Bohemia. One day, it is said, they will rise under his leadership and return to rid the nation of its enemies. During antigovernment demonstrations in November 1989, the statue of Saint Wenceslas became a shrine to the people. On the night the resignation of the Communist Party's general secretary was announced, some people chanted, "The knights of Blaník have arrived!"

emperor in Constantinople sent two monks to introduce Christianity in the region.

The missionaries, Constantine (later renamed Cyril) and his brother, Methodius, arrived in 863. As part of their missionary work in the region, they not only preached in Slavic, but also translated the Bible into the Slavic language then in use. To do this, Cyril created the Slavic alphabet that later developed into the Cyrillic alphabet. Their work was the first example of Slavic in written form.

The Romans named Bohemia after a fifth-century B.C. Celtic group, the Boii—Boiohemum in Latin.

THE PŘEMYSL DYNASTY

According to tradition, the Přemysl (PRZHE-mysl) dynasty was founded in A.D. 800 by Přemysl, who started as a humble farm laborer. By 950 the German king Otto I had conquered Bohemia and made it part of the Holy

Roman Empire. The Přemysl dynasty ruled Bohemia on the German kings' behalf until it fell in 1306 with the assassination of Wenceslas III. In the later years of the dynasty, the Přemysls were responsible for uniting the groups of Bohemia and solidifying the region's conversion to Christianity.

The Přemysl dynasty was succeeded by the Luxembourg dynasty, whose first ruler was John of Luxembourg.

BOHEMIA'S GOLDEN AGE

Bohemia's golden age occurred under the eldest son of John of Luxembourg, also named Wenceslas. He changed his name to Charles and ruled from 1346 to 1378. In 1355 Charles was crowned emperor in Rome, and Prague was chosen as capital of the Holy Roman Empire. As a result, Prague grew to become one of Europe's most important cities politically and culturally, attracting French, Italian, and German scholars, architects, scientists, and artists.

During Charles VI's reign several of Prague's most significant Gothic buildings were constructed, including Saint Vitus Cathedral and Charles

The eastern facade of Saint Vitus Cathedral in Prague, the largest cathedral in the Czech Republic.

THE HUSSITE REFORM MOVEMENT

The Hussite Movement was named after Jan Hus (1369?—1415). Hus studied liberal arts (a group of seven disciplines in medieval universities) and divinity at Charles University, began lecturing there in 1398, and was appointed rector of the university in 1403. In 1402 he also became a preacher at Bethlehem Chapel, where he led a movement against corruption in the church. Hus demanded a return to early Christian doctrines and practices, such as the celebration of communion with both bread and wine. The university did not support the outspoken Hus, and the archbishop of Prague and Pope John XXIII strongly refuted his doctrines. He was summoned to the Council of Constance in Baden, Germany—the seat of the bishop of the region—to recant the views he was alleged to hold. Jan Hus refused, and after being condemned for heresy, he was burned at the stake on July 6, 1415.

Hus's execution ignited two decades of religious and civil war. Bohemia became strongly anti-Catholic during those Hussite Wars, and even after the fighting stopped, the dominion remained independent of the Holy Roman Empire for another two centuries.

University. The stone Charles Bridge, which he ordered built, is still the main link today between the east and west banks of the capital.

Charles had a great gift for diplomacy, and during his reign there was harmony between the church, the throne, and the nobility. His son, Wenceslas IV, lacked the conciliatory gift of his father. During his rule a reform movement grew, led by Jan Hus, the rector at Bethlehem Chapel. The chapel is significant for another reason—its services were conducted exclusively in Czech.

THE HAPSBURG DYNASTY

Many Germans settled in Bohemia during the Přemysl dynasty.

The Hapsburgs (also spelled Habsburg), a German royal family whose name derives from the Hapsburg Castle in Switzerland, provided rulers for the Holy Roman Empire, Austria, and Spain. In 1526 Ferdinand I of Hapsburg took up the Czech throne, thus promoting the Hapsburg rule over the country that lasted until 1918. Ferdinand reinstated Catholicism in the country. The seat of power was moved to Vienna, and Prague became less significant for the Hapsburgs. Rudolf II, Holy Roman Emperor, was crowned the Czech king in 1576, and he moved his court back to Prague in 1583. This move reestablished Prague as the seat of the empire once again.

The Hapsburgs, however, failed to fulfill their promise of religious tolerance. Indignant over that, but perhaps even more so over the loss of traditional privileges, the Protestant Czech upper classes provoked what came to be known as the Thirty Years' War. The war left Bohemia's economy in ruins and spread destruction across much of Central Europe. The Protestant Czechs were defeated at the Battle of the White Mountain in 1620. The battle consolidated Hapsburg rule and stripped the Czechs of their independence, individual rights and property, and religious freedom. The Protestants were forced to become Catholics. When the Hapsburgs moved the capital back to Vienna, Prague was reduced, culturally and economically, to a sluggish provincial town for more than a century.

The king's representatives being thrown out the window of the Bohemian chancellery, marking the start of the Thirty Years' War (1618-48).

THE CZECH NATIONAL REVIVAL MOVEMENT

Nationalist sentiments swept through much of Europe during the late 18th and early 19th centuries. With more Czechs educated—thanks to the educational reforms instituted by the Hapsburg empress Maria Theresa—a vocal, better informed middle class emerged. Economic reforms forced native Czech laborers into bigger towns, diminishing the influence of the German minorities there.

The revival movement in Prague found expression in literature, theater, and journalism. The leaders of the movement were not political figures but historians and linguists, and the key issues at first were the rights of Czechs to speak and develop a literature in their own language. Although they had been defeated, Czechs continued to push for political independence and the right to use their own language.

THE FIRST REPUBLIC

Many Czechs and Slovaks fought against the Germans and Austrians during World War I. On October 28, 1918, an independent Czechoslovak republic, called the First Republic, was proclaimed with the support of the Allied nations. Prague was designated its capital city and Tomáš Garrigue Masaryk its first president. It was ruled by a coalition of Czech and Slovak parties, and its charter guaranteed equal rights to all citizens. Today, Czechs proudly refer to the First Republic as the only liberal democracy at that time in Central Europe.

THE DARK DAYS OF WORLD WAR II

By the 1930s, 3 million German speakers lived in Bohemia and most succumbed to Adolf Hitler's twisted vision of a grander Germany. The British and French governments pressured Czechoslovakia into giving up Sudetenland, the northwest region of Bohemia adjoining Germany. They believed that such sacrifice would appease Hitler and avoid a war. Opposing the move, President Edvard Beneš of Czechoslovakia resigned on October 5, 1938, and went into exile, first in London, then in Chicago.

As history demonstrates, Hitler was not appeased. On March 14, 1939, Slovakia was also annexed. The next day the Germans occupied Bohemia and Moravia, which the Nazis named the Protectorate of Bohemia and Moravia of the Third Reich. In the period of Nazi repression that followed, Jews were targeted, but other Czechs did not escape persecution. In May 1942, after the assassination of Reinhard Heydrich, a Nazi persecutor, by unknown attackers, the Gestapo (abbreviation of Geheime Staatspolizei, German for Secret State Police) shot to death all the male inhabitants of the mining village of Lidice, accusing them of sheltering the assassins. The women were sent to concentration camps, and the surviving children were parceled out to German families.

In the first two years of the First Republic, issues about the borders separating the republic from Austria, Germany, and Poland were resolved.

Edvard Beneš (*right*) was the foreign minister before succeeding Tomáš Masaryk (*left*) in 1935 to become the president.

As a result of talks between the exiles, including Edvard Beneš and the Soviet Union, the Red Army had great influence on the Czechoslovakian underground movement against the Germans. On May 5, 1945, the common people rose up against the German occupiers, and by May 8, after fierce fighting, most of Prague had been liberated. U.S. forces arrived first but allowed the Soviet army to enter Prague as its liberator on May 9.

Until World War II, Czechoslovakia had enjoyed the 10th-highest standard of living in the world. By the end of the 1980s, the standard had plunged to 42nd place, well below many third world countries.

POSTWAR COMMUNISM

Edvard Beneš returned to Czechoslovakia as president in 1945. In the 1946 election the Communist Party was the dominant party in the coalition group that formed the government, with Klement Gottwald as prime minister. Tensions soon developed between communist and noncommunist cabinet members.

Girls from the Czech Youth Group helping to clear the rubble and to rebuild Prague City Hall after World War II.

The Warsaw Pact was a "treaty of friendship, cooperation, and mutual assistance" between the Soviet Union, Albania, Bulgaria, Czechoslovakia, East Germany, Hungary, Poland, and Romania. The treaty lasted from 1955 to 1991. Albania quit it in 1968, and East Germany stepped out in 1990. The Warsaw Pact had enabled the Soviet Union to maintain its army in those countries.

In January 1948 the Communist Party took over the government by force, with the military backing of the Soviet Union. A new constitution was devised in May, giving the Communist Party total control. President Beneš resigned rather than sanction it, and Gottwald was elected president by the Federal Assembly in June 1948. Industry and agriculture were soon nationalized. Thousands of people fled the country, and many leading figures in Czechoslovak society were imprisoned, executed, or died in labor camps. The 1950s was an era of harsh political repression and economic decline.

PRAGUE SPRING

Civil liberties increased and censorship practices were loosened during the 1960s, especially toward the end of that decade under the new president, Alexander Dubček. That period of restored freedoms is known as the Prague Spring. Soviet-bloc leaders became very agitated by the Czech moves toward a realized democracy, and on August 21, 1968, Warsaw Pact troops and tanks invaded the country.

Slovak President, Ivan Gasparovic (right), and Austrian president, Heinz Fischer (left), commemorate the 40th anniversary of the end of the Prague Spring communist reform movement in 1968 at a memorial for Prague Spring leader Alexander Dubček in 2008.

In the following decade thousands of Communist Party members were expelled from the party and lost their jobs. Many professionals and other educated civilians were forced to earn their living doing menial jobs. That was followed in the 1980s by economic and political stagnation, corruption of the state system, and severely lowered living standards—all of which contributed to a growing dissatisfaction with the communist regime.

THE VELVET REVOLUTION

In 1977 the country's intellectuals signed a petition known as Charter 77, listing their grievances against the repressive communist regime. It failed in producing changes, but in the decade that followed, members of that group played an important role in fomenting dissatisfaction against the regime. Toward the end of 1989, the citizens of Czechoslovakia began expressing strong discontent with the communist regime.

Czechs light candles at a memorial of the Velvet Revolution.

The first of several demonstrations took place on August 21, 1989, the 21st anniversary of the crushing of the Prague Spring. The demonstrators—a mix of young and old, intellectuals and laborers—sang the national anthem and waved the national flag as they demanded freedom of expression, thought, association, and belief. Censorship had controlled all aspects of their lives. They wanted the freedom to decide what music to play and what books to read without fear of government reprisal.

On November 17, 1989, the anniversary of the death of nine students killed by the Nazis in 1939, Prague's communist youth organized an officially sanctioned demonstration in Wenceslas Square in Prague. That venerated square, the symbolic heart of the country, is presided over by the statue of Wenceslas, the country's patron saint.

The students declared an indefinite strike and were joined by actors and musicians. Although that was a peaceful protest, riot police were sent in to suppress the students. As a result, a week of demonstrations followed in Prague in which, in a city of 2 million, over 750,000 people participated. On

November 27, 10 days after the student strike, a general strike was held; over half the population stopped working for two hours.

The strike precipitated the resignation of the communist chairperson of the Federal Assembly and heralded the collapse of the communist government. On December 28, 1989, Václav Havel was elected president, Václav Klaus was elected prime minister, and Alexander Dubček became the speaker of parliament. The days that followed came to be called the Velvet Revolution because there were no casualties. The shameful aspect of its "bloodless" nature is that communist leaders were not prosecuted for their crimes.

Following the overthrow of communism, the Havel government had two main objectives: to ensure the first free elections since 1946 and to make a rapid push toward a free-market economy. That process involved the return of property to its original owners (pre-1948) and the privatization of most state-owned industry.

Former Czech president and playwright, Václav Havel.

Czechs in general were more in favor of radical economic reform than the Slovaks, because the Slovaks were suffering greater economic hardship and higher unemployment from a declining arms industry. Another deep-rooted issue was the resentment the Slovaks felt at having been treated as second-class citizens for many decades. Those sentiments were fueled by the election of the Movement for a Democratic Slovakia party in June 1992 in Slovakia. The party leader, Vladimír Mečiar, was a strong supporter of complete independence for Slovaks and slower economic reform. The Civic Democratic Party won the election in the Czech lands. During postelection negotiations between the two parties, Václav Klaus, leader of the Civic Democratic Party, insisted on separation.

Since the breakup of Czechoslovakia, the Czech Republic has mainly enjoyed positive consequences of economic reform, including booming tourism, a solid industrial base, low unemployment, stores full of merchandise, and the restoration of city buildings. There have been, nonetheless, some negative impacts of embracing a capitalistic economy, including an acute housing shortage, steeply rising crime, severe pollution, and a deteriorating health system.

THE VELVET DIVORCE

President Václav Havel resigned in protest, refusing to preside over the split. In the first few months of independence, relations between the two republics were determined by 25 interstate treaties that provided a framework for issues such as the division of property, federal institutions, and a common currency. Prague became the capital of the Czech Republic, Václav Havel was once again elected the president, and Václav Klaus became prime minister.

AFTER INDEPENDENCE

The Czech Republic became a member of the North Atlantic Treaty Organization (NATO) on March 12, 1999, and joined the European Union (EU) on May 1, 2004. Both events are significant landmarks in the nation's history. The country is also a member of the United Nations and the World Trade Organization.

Although the Czech Republic has achieved a great deal since its independence, the government still faces important challenges in many areas, including completing its economic restructuring, eliminating corruption, improving its environmental performance, and reforming its failed health service as well as retooling its pensions program.

Czech President Václav Klaus (right) holding a press conference with European Commission President José Manuel Barroso (left) in 2009 in Prague.

The Czech Republic's most recent general elections, in 2006, resulted in a deadlock, leaving not one of the political parties involved—the Christian Democrats (KDU–ČSL), the Social Democrats (ČSSD), the Civic Democratic Party (ODS), the Communists (KSČM), and the Greens (SZ)—strong enough to form a majority government. The impasse was resolved, however, in January 2007, when the center-right coalition (ODS and KDU–ČSL) and the Greens joined hands to finally win the right to govern.

The Czech Republic is due to host the rotating EU presidency in 2009, which will allow it to significantly influence the policies of the European Union.

GOVERNMENT

The town hall in Přemysl Otakar II Square of Old Town, in Náméstí Přemysla.

CHAPTER 3

FROM 1948 UNTIL 1989 THE FORMER Republic of Czechoslovakia was a communist state with a one-party system (a single political party forms the government, while no other parties are permitted to run candidates for election). Since the overthrow of the communist regime in 1989, the Czechs and Slovaks have gone their separate ways, after 74 years of joint statehood. The Czech Republic officially began its political, judicial, and civil life on January 1, 1993, as an independent state based on a system of parliamentary democracy.

When the Czech Republic was still a common state with the Slovaks (as Czechoslovakia), it was ruled as a communist state. The communist rule, however, under immense pressure from its people, eventually fell and Czechoslovakia separated. On January 1, 1993, the Czech Republic gained its independence and was run under a system of parliamentary democracy from then on.

WHO IS IN POWER?

The president is the head of state and is elected for a term of five years. The prime minister and the cabinet, though, wield the greater power. The prime minister is chosen by the president and advises the president on the selection of the other cabinet members. The cabinet consists of the prime minister, deputy prime ministers, and ministers.

THE PREAMBLE OF THE CONSTITUTION

"We, the citizens of the Czech Republic in Bohemia, Moravia, and Silesia, at this time of the reconstitution of an independent Czech State, true to all the sound traditions of the ancient statehood of the Lands of the Czech Crown as well as of Czechoslovak statehood, resolve to build, protect, and advance the Czech Republic in the spirit of the inalienable values of human dignity and freedom as the home of equal and free citizens who are aware of their obligations toward others and of their responsibility to the community."

Václav Klaus (red tie) and his cabinet of ministers in Prague's Hradcany Castle. The president was re-elected in 2008.

Industry and Trade; Justice; Education, Youth and Sports; Interior and Informatics; Foreign Affairs; Health; and Agriculture and Environment.

The Czech Republic is divided into Prague, its capital city, and 13 administrative centers: Středočeský kraj (Central Bohemia), Jihočeský kraj (South Bohemia), Plzečský kraj (Pilsen), Karlovarský kraj, Ústecký kraj, Liberecký kraj, Královéhradecký kraj, Pardubický kraj, Vysočina, Jihomoravský kraj, Olomoucký kraj, Zlínský kraj, Moravskoslezský kraj.

A NEW CONSTITUTION

The Czech National Council adopted the constitution of the Czech Republic, establishing the country as a parliamentary democracy, on December 16, 1992. It came into effect January 1, 1993, coinciding with the commencement of the new republic. Many of its Western liberal principles are similar to those of the constitution for the noncommunist, post-1989 federation of Czechoslovakia, which was written in a very difficult period, amid tension and differences of opinion between Czech and Slovakian leaders. The Czechs have enshrined in their constitution their solemn desire for democracy and freedom, as well as their recognition of their responsibilities as individual citizens and as a community.

The Old Town Hall, built around 1240, is the oldest secular monument in Brno, the second-largest city in the Czech Republic.

The process of forming the constitution began in the June 1990 elections that decided the political leadership: the Civic Forum movement headed by Václav Havel and the Slovakian leader, Vladimír Mečiar. Apart from writing the new constitution, the emerging government had to make economic plans and consider untried directions in foreign policy. When it became clear that there would be little consensus in economic reform and that territorial separation was inevitable, Havel resigned in the summer of 1992 and the Civic Forum fell apart. Meanwhile, by June 1991, Soviet troops that were part of the Warsaw Pact had withdrawn from Czechoslovakia.

THE HOUSES OF PARLIAMENT

The constitution allows for a parliament with two chambers: the senate (or upper house) and the chamber of deputies. Czech citizens aged 18 years and older have the right to vote.

The chamber of deputies consists of 200 deputies, each of whom is elected for a term of four years. Elections are held by secret ballot and according to proportional representation. Czech citizens aged 21 and older are eligible to be elected to the chamber of deputies.

The Czech government functioned without an upper house from January 1993 until late 1995 when the senate came into being in time for the 1996 election. The senate now has 81 senators. Every two years, one-third of the senators are elected for a term of six years. Senators are elected by secret

The Czech national flag proudly flies at the Baroque-style building of the Presidential Office.

ballot according to the principles of the majority system. Czech citizens 40 years of age and older may be elected to the senate.

A CONTROVERSIAL SYMBOL

The traditional flag of the Czech lands had two equal horizontal bands of white and red. Because this is identical to the flags of other former Soviet bloc countries, the Czech Republic chose to use the flag of the First Republic, which has an isosceles triangle of blue, with its base on the hoist side, wedged into the two horizontal bands. This choice raised a storm of controversy with Slovakia, for the two republics had already agreed not to use the old federal symbols.

JUDICIARY

The judicial system is determined by a law enacted in July 1991, which allows for the establishment of a 15-member constitutional court and a supreme administrative court. The president appoints the judges of the supreme and constitutional courts, and the senate approves or rejects his nominations.

There are civil, criminal, commercial, and administrative courts. When disputes are related to business, the people concerned go to a commercial court to settle matters. Administrative courts are courts of appeal for citizens who question the legality of decisions made in state institutions.

The courts under the Ministry of Justice have a clear hierarchy: they are at republic, regional, and district levels. The first point of appeal is the district court, where cases are usually decided by a panel consisting of a judge and two associate judges. Associate judges are citizens of good standing over the age of 24, elected for four years. The regional courts deal with more serious cases and also may act as courts of appeal for district courts. In both district and regional courts, a single judge rather than a panel of judges will occasionally decide these cases.

Mandatory national conscription was abolished in the Czech Republic in 2004.

Military courts are convened under the jurisdiction of the Ministry of Defense. The supreme court interprets the law, acts as a guide to other courts, and also functions as a court of appeal.

MILITARY FORCES

Compulsory military service was abolished at the close of 2004, ending 140 years of military obligation for Czech men.

Under the communist regime, military strength was approximately 200,000 personnel on active duty. The Czech Republic has reduced the number of its military personnel to approximately 30,000. Besides the army and air force, there are also civil defense, railroad, and internal security units. The president of the republic is the military commander-in-chief. The 2006 defense budget for the Czech Republic was $2.5 billion, compared with $535 billion for the United States.

Dividing the troops in the former federal army, as part of the partition process, was a formidable task. Stationing troops along the Czech-Slovak border is prohibited.

ECONOMY

Czechs harvesting hops in Zatec. The Czech Republic is one the world's largest exporters of hops, used in making malt liquors.

CHAPTER 4

TODAY, THE CZECH REPUBLIC IS ONE of the most stable and successful post-communist countries in all of Europe. In 2007 the real growth rate was estimated to be 6.5 percent. The Czech Republic's economy has experienced many fundamental changes since the communist regime ended in 1989. In 1990 the finance minister of Czechoslovakia, Václav Klaus (later to be prime minister of the Czech Republic and current president), instigated a wide-ranging series of reforms designed to bring about a free-market economy.

The Czech Republic's industrial base includes the production of steel, iron, cement, ceramics, plastics, cotton, clothing, and beer. The timber industry provides most of the wood required for newsprint, furniture, plywood, and traditional woodworking. As of June 2006, 60 percent of all Czech forests are state owned, 15.4 percent are communal forests, 23.1 percent are privately owned and 1.5 percent are forest cooperatives.

TWO PHASES OF REFORM

While he was prime minister, Václav Klaus instigated a two-phase privatization plan. The first phase required the return of property to

When the Czech Republic officially became an independent state, it also became a member of the International Monetary Fund, the World Bank, the European Bank for Reconstruction and Development, and the Conference on Security and Cooperation in Europe. The footsteps to capitalism had set out in earnest.

MIREK TOPOLÁNEK, THE PRIME MINISTER

Mirek Topolánek is the current prime minister of the Czech Republic. He has served as chairperson of the right-wing Civic Democratic Party since November 2002, succeeding Václav Klaus, now the sitting president of the Czech Republic.

Born May 15, 1956, in Vsetín, Mirek Topolánek attended a military high school. He obtained a degree in mechanical engineering from Brno University of Technology. Topolánek is the cofounder of the engineering company VAE Ltd., which was set up in 1991.

Topolánek joined the Civic Forum in 1989, and has been a member of the Civic Democratic Party since 1994. He served in the senate from 1996 to 2004 and as its deputy chairperson from 2002 to 2004. He has also been a member of the Chamber of Deputies since 2006.

Václav Klaus appointed Topolánek prime minister in August 2006. Topolánek's first cabinet failed to gain the approval of the Chamber of Deputies. By January 2007, however, he had formed a right-wing coalition government composed of members of the Green Party and the Christian and Democratic Union who together formed the Czechoslovak People's Party.

In October 2007 Topolánek launched his Five Prime Minister's Priorities, which included the following major programs: Healthy Public Finances, Modern and Efficient State, Safe Citizen in a Safe Country, Removing Barriers, and Promoting Science and Education.

Mirek Topolánek is separated from his wife, Pavla Topoláneková. He has four children.

pre-1948 owners, or their descendants, and called for the sale of enterprises through auctions or directly to foreign buyers. That phase has been quite successful, with almost 16,500 units privatized and 183 units returned to former owners. Over 80 percent of enterprises have been privatized. Today, most restaurants, hotels, and retail stores are privately owned, while the government still owns some theaters, museums, and castles. Many banks that were state-run have been privatized. There are now both local and international banks with branches in the Czech Republic.

The entrance at Czech Republic's third-largest bank, Investicni Postovni Banka.

The second phase of the plan concentrated on large-scale industries and small enterprises that had not found buyers. A coupon system was introduced to give every citizen a chance to become a shareholder. After January 1994 the coupons could be exchanged for shares in over 770 unsold companies. The idea was accepted enthusiastically by most Czechs and Slovaks at the time, with 8.5 million people buying coupons. This phase also focused on the return of confiscated property to the Catholic Church, the implementation of a bankruptcy law, and the privatization of agriculture and health care.

Of the total labor force, almost 60 percent work in service categories and 38 percent in industry. The number of people employed in agriculture has decreased dramatically.

AGRICULTURE IN DECLINE

Agriculture presents one of the biggest problems facing the government today. Crop production has declined since the late 1980s. Under communism, land that had been private property became state property and was

Workers prepare to plant potatoes in the Elbe River region. Potatoes are one of Czech Republic's main exports.

exhaustively overcultivated. Communism guaranteed farmers a wage, no matter how much they produced, so they did not have to work efficiently. Since the farm they worked was state owned, they did not have to make it commercially worthwhile. Consequently, a farm machinery breakdown was seen as lucky, as the farmer could not work at all until the equipment was repaired—and repairs often took weeks.

Today, many Czechs cannot claim their land because it is impossible to determine which section of it was once theirs. Many are reluctant to make a claim, anyway, because to make the land financially viable will require much effort and investment. Ironically, many owners of small plots are joining cooperatives in order to make a living. It will be many years before the land becomes productive once again, and there is still a shortage of appropriate technology on the smaller farms.

AN ECONOMIC REPORT CARD

Although the Czech Republic weathered a rocky economic path after the Velvet Divorce, the republic has now successfully embraced the new market economy. Today it is one of the most prosperous former communist states. The economic growth rate in 2007 was estimated as 6.5 percent, though it was expected to slow to 4 percent in 2008 because of the global financial crisis.

The Czech Republic's recent growth has been mainly due to exports to the other EU countries, such as Germany. There is also growing domestic demand among the Czech people for all kinds of products, from automotives to home mortgages. Their exposure to credit cards has also contributed to greater demand for goods and services.

By 2010 the current government intends to reduce the budget deficit to 2.3 percent of gross domestic product (GDP). In order to achieve that target, they have planned to cut back social welfare spending and reform the tax system. The present government is also working toward meeting the criteria for adoption of the euro by 2012.

Although the country has ample fertile land and resources, it is still not self-sufficient in food production. A basic problem is organization and distribution. Fruit on the trees in the countryside remains unpicked, while grapes imported from Spain are sold in the city streets. It may be simply a question of time before agriculture absorbs the effects of rapid economic change and of the reduced labor force to become a successful sector again.

The major crops are sugar beets, wheat, potatoes, corn, barley, rye, and hops. The preferred livestock are cattle, pigs, chickens, and horses. The dairy industry continues to supply most domestic requirements. South Bohemia has a well-established fish-farm industry, consisting mainly of carp cultivation. Remarkably, these carp lakes were excavated during the Middle Ages. Carp is a traditional dish at Christmas.

RESOURCES AND ENERGY

There are limited reserves of coal, coke, timber, uranium, and iron ore in the Czech Republic. Central Bohemia, between Prague and Plzeň, is an important

In south Czech Republic, the discovery of copper, gold, and silver deposits resulted in the development and growth of mining communities.

region for iron ore mining. Lead and zinc ore are mined near Kutná Hora and Příbram in Bohemia and in the northeast of the country; uranium in Příbram and in the northern regions of Bohemia; and tin in the Ore Mountains to the northeast.

The major centers for coal mining and manufacturing traditionally have been in the northern regions of Bohemia. Severe air pollution, a side effect of burning low-quality brown coal (lignite), is a serious problem there. At present, most electricity comes from coal-burning plants and the nuclear reactor at Dukovany. Oil and natural gas are imported from Russia. To reduce fuel dependency on Russia, an oil pipeline through Germany was constructed, and a nuclear power plant opened in 2002 at Temelín. That was a communist project that the post-1989 government decided to complete, modifying the original Soviet design with Western safety technology and procedures. The controversial project has been the focus of protests by antinuclear activists, including some overseas environmentalists. In 2006 plans to expand this plant were suspended in an attempt to discourage the use of nuclear energy.

TRANSPORTATION

TRAINS AND BUSES The Czech Republic has an extremely comprehensive railway infrastructure that stretches 75 miles (120 km) of railroads per 386 square miles (1,000 square km) of the country. Czech Railways owns and operates approximately 5,894 miles (9,483 km) of railway lines. Over 180 million passengers and over 110 million tons (100 million metric tonnes) of goods are transported annually by Czech railways.

Streetcars in the central area are typical of bigger towns in the republic. Prague also has an extensive subway system; smaller towns have a bus system and many have trolley-buses.

The state railway company was dissolved after the Velvet Divorce. Today, improvements continue to be made to the network, including the connection of core rails to main European lines, meeting the requirements of EU standards as well as improving safety, speed, and reliability.

Buses and streetcars tend to be cheap and fast. Buses connect the suburbs to city centers; some cover even longer distances. Commuters in Prague have the option of traveling by subway. Commuters purchase train, subway, streetcar, and bus tickets at tobacco stands, newsstands, and ticket-vending machines in the larger cities. Timetables for public transportation can also be purchased at bookstores.

ON THE ROAD The republic has a network of good roads. The Czech highway system, made up of motorways (superhighways) and high-speed roads, is continually being developed and improved. As it stands, more than 620 miles (1,000 km) of these roads are open. When completed, the total distance will extend to 1,305 miles (2,100 km). Some of the more important motorways include Motorway D1 that connects Prague to Brno; Motorway D5 that connects Prague, Plzeň, and Rozvadov; and Motorway D11 from Prague to Kolín. An electronic toll system was launched in 2007. This toll applies to all vehicles, except motorcycles, that use motorways, expressways, and certain other roads. All vehicles subject to the toll are required to be equipped with an electronic device that collects the necessary fee from a prepaid account while the vehicle passes through the tollgate. An increasing number of Czechs own cars, which means that highways and country roads now have heavier traffic than they used to. As in the rest of Europe and the United States, vehicles are driven on the right side of the road. The legal driving age is 18. Penalties for speeding and drunk driving are very high. The theft of cars and valuables from cars has become a major problem in the larger cities.

A sleek jet at the Czech Republic's Prague-Ruzyne Airport.

IN THE AIR There are four big international airports: Prague, Ostrava, Brno, and Karlovy Vary. The Prague-Ruzyne International Airport is by far the biggest airport in the Czech Republic. It serves more than 11 million passengers and provides space for 203,000 aircraft every year. The airport serves more than 100 national and international destinations. A new terminal, Sever 2 (North 2), was opened in January 2006. By 2010 the Prague airport expects to have completed a new parallel landing runway.

BOATS Boat transportation in the Czech Republic makes use of several large rivers: the Elbe (the Labe), the Vltava (the lower reaches), and the Berounka. Among other rivers that can be used are some stretches of the Morava, Bečva, and Odra. Boats are used mainly for transporting freight throughout the country. Traveling by boat is popular in Prague among visitors, as the many waterways promise interesting sightseeing.

Many tourists opt to take in the sights of Prague via cruise boats.

ENVIRONMENT

A meadow and surrounding forest at Sumava National Park.

CHAPTER 5

Today the Czech Republic's environment is under threat from air, water, and land pollution caused by industrial and mining activities. Toxic rains have damaged its forests and a number of its fauna have been listed as endangered. Fortunately, the presence of numerous national parks are ensuring the preservation of the country's plant and animal life.

PARTS OF THE REPUBLIC ARE among the most polluted areas in the world. The concentration of light industry in northern Bohemia and Moravia since the industrial revolution has been exacerbated by the introduction of heavy industry during the communist years. The burning of low-grade brown coal is primarily responsible for the 1,542,800 tons (1,400,000 metric tonnes) of sulfur that industry emits annually. Acid rain has affected 60 percent of all the forests in the country.

Prague is the site of some of the worst air pollution in the country. In the winter, when people are using their home furnaces and power plants are running at peak production, pollution often reaches dangerous levels.

According to World Bank statistics, 3 percent of deaths in the Czech Republic are due to air pollution, while child deaths due to respiratory diseases are 2.4 times higher in polluted areas than in unpolluted ones. In the past, public attention tended to be focused more on creating a better standard of living than on the environment.

Since the passing in the senate in 2004 of a bill on improving air quality, however, the government is working hard to reduce the emission levels at more than a hundred major polluters in order to meet European Union criteria.

Wild grass around a gentle stream in Zvonkova, Šumava National Park.

small number of national parks and forests are under careful supervision. These include the primeval forests of Boubín, Mionší, Bílá Opava, Ranšpurk, Žofín, and Trojmezí. A few others are regarded as jewels of Czech nature and important subjects of scientific research. Conserving these beautiful areas is essential to maintain the biodiversity of the region. There are 24 national parks that have been established as Protected Landscape Areas. The main ones are the Krkonoše, Šumava, Podyjí, and České Švýcarsko national parks.

Šumava National Park is located in the Plzeň and South Bohemian regions of the Czech Republic along the border with Germany and Austria. The Šumava Range is made up of the most extensive forest in Central Europe. It is covered mainly with spruce trees. It is possible to see lynx in this beautiful area.

Krkonoše National Park is a UNESCO Biosphere Reserve site. It is located in the Liberec and Hradec Králové regions and lies in the Czech Republic's highest mountain range, the Krkonoše Mountains.

Podyjí National Park is located in the South Moravian region. This unique park is home to primeval forests. The České Švýcarsko National Park was established in January 2000 and shares a border with Germany.

A red deer in Šumava National Park and Protected Landscape Area.

FLORA AND FAUNA

Almost 70 percent of the Czech forest is home to mixed or deciduous flora and a large variety of fauna. Some original steppe grassland areas are still found in the region of Moravia, but today most of these lowlands have been cultivated.

Mammals that are commonly found in the Czech Republic include the fox, hare, deer, rabbit, and wild pig. A variety of birds inhabit the Czech lowlands and valleys. Fish such as carp, pike, and trout are found in most rivers and natural and man-made ponds.

Many important improvements have been made to the environment in recent years. As a result, some species of plants and animals are starting to reappear after many years' absence in nature, ranging from mushrooms and lichens to vertebrates. The Czech Republic belongs to the NATURA 2000 network that aims to maintain and restore the populations of species and their natural habitats.

ENDANGERED SPECIES

In spite of the many positive changes being made to the Czech environment, sadly, some types of animals and plants are disappearing from the country altogether. There are many reasons for this, some of them unknown. Many believe, however, that one of the main causes may be the deliberate destruction inflicted by man.

The endangered list, compiled in 2001 by the International Union for Conservation of Nature (IUCN), includes seven mammal species, six bird species, six types of freshwater fish, and seven plant species.

Endangered species include the Atlantic sturgeon, slender-billed curlew, and Spengler's freshwater mussel. Other vulnerable animals include the Bechstein's bat, Eurasian otter, European squirrel, garden dormouse, Geoffroy's bat, lesser horseshoe bat, pond bat, and the Western barbastelle bat.

ECOTOURISM

Like many other countries that fortunately have areas of outstanding natural beauty, the Czech Republic has started to promote its green, or ecotourism, programs. These invite the visitor to enjoy local nature, forests, and wildlife flora and fauna. Moreover, ecotourism ensures that the detrimental aspects of conventional tourism on the Czech environment are minimized. Popular ecotours include cycling, hiking, and bird-watching.

Tourists take in the natural beauty of Kamenice Canyon by boat.

WATER

The long-term annual average precipitation in the Czech Republic is equal to about 26 inches (672 mm). The republic has a total of 3.6 cubic miles (15 cubic km) of freshwater resources. More than half of the water, some 57 percent, is used for industry and only 1 percent is used for farming. Czechs in urban and rural areas everywhere have access to safe drinking water.

Since 1991 the main Czech watercourses, including the Elbe, Vltava, Morava, Dyje, and Oder, have maintained good water quality. Nevertheless, certain rivers, such as the Jihlava, Lužnice, and Bílina, carry extremely polluted water, though improvements are being made to make the water safer for swimming and water sports.

POLLUTION

The Czech Republic suffers from a poor history of pollution, with air, water, and land pollution among the highest in the EU. This has been caused mainly by industry, mining, and agriculture. In some parts of the country where pollution levels are excessive, there is a high percentage of residents who have become afflicted with lung cancer and other diseases caused by their contaminated surroundings.

AIR POLLUTION Parts of the Czech Republic are among the most polluted in the world. The concentration of light industry in northern Bohemia and Moravia since the industrial revolution has been exacerbated by the introduction of heavy industry during the communist years. The contamination of the republic's air is a result of the widespread use of lignite as a source of energy during the communist era. The levels of sulfur dioxide that were emitted were some of the highest in the whole of Europe. The burning of the low-grade brown coal is primarily responsible for the 1,543,236 tons (1,400,000 metric tonnes) of sulfur that industry emits annually. Acid rain has affected 60 percent of all the forests in the country. The situation so concerned the other Western European countries that they offered financial help to encourage Czechs to try to reduce their

Plumes of smoke being emitted from the nuclear power plant in Temelin.

migrating pollution. Large strides were made in the 1990s to improve their air pollution profile.

Prague is the site of some of the worst air pollution in the country. In the winter, when more energy is expended to provide heating for people, the pollution can shoot up to very dangerous levels.

These dangerous levels of air pollution can lead to respiratory illnesses that may ultimately lead to death. In the past, public attention tended to be more focused on creating a better standard of living than on the environment. To meet European criteria, in 2004 the senate passed a law on improving air quality, and the government is working hard to cut emission levels from over a hundred major polluters.

Air pollution in the Czech Republic has improved during the last decade as a result of a decreasing consumption of brown coal, with its high content of sulfur dioxide, used in large power plants. As in other parts of Europe, Czech air pollution is also made worse by toxic traffic emissions.

While the Czech Republic enjoys cleaner air and reduced levels of smog today, some regions still suffer from poor air conditions. In other regions, it should be noted that the air quality is better than in some other EU countries.

WATER POLLUTION As a result of over 300 new wastewater treatment plants that have been installed in larger cities and towns, the quality of water has improved tremendously. According to the Czech National Standard, however, a third of the water of all watercourses is still considered highly polluted, so much critical work remains to be done.

LAND EROSION The decrease in mining of brown and black coal has put a stop to the devastation of the natural landscape of the North Bohemian and Sokolov brown coal-mining areas. Similarly, a reduction in uranium mining has gradually improved conditions in western Bohemia. The Czech Republic also suffers from significant land erosion brought about by poor agricultural and mining practices.

NOISE POLLUTION The number of vehicles using Czech roads is increasing rapidly. This growth inevitably leads to a rise in the noise and air pollution levels. The shift from using public transportation—trains, streetcars, and buses—to using cars will undoubtedly generate negative consequences for the environment, especially increased air pollution.

Although all types of pollution continue to be an obstinate problem in the Czech Republic, the people and the government together are working hard to rectify the situation. In fact, many improvements have been made in just the past decade.

The clean streets of Prague's Old Town Square. There has been a striking improvement in the cleanliness of the streets of the Czech Republic.

THE MODERN CZECH LANDSCAPE

In the last ten years, the Czech Republic has experienced many changes at a rapid pace. As a result, little time was given to the proper planning, for example, of new buildings. Czech towns and cities today are usually blighted by buildings of a poor quality. The sudden building boom, brought about partly by the changes to the economy, has inadvertently but adversely affected the Czech rural and urban environment.

A positive change is that in many cities, large towns, and municipalities today, there is a noticeable improvement in the cleanliness of public areas and streets. Nonetheless, there still exist numerous unlicensed dumps, and unsightly litter is seen in many areas of larger cities.

Many Czech cities and towns are becoming more built-up and cramped with new buildings and defiled by advertising billboards. The areas at the edges of many towns and cities, which used to be farmland, are now being used as industrial and commercial zones. Unfortunately, there are also many unoccupied buildings that are slowly deteriorating and other properties that simply have been abandoned.

WASTE MANAGEMENT

Some parts of the Czech Republic continue to practice unacceptable means of waste management. Many illegal waste dumps are still eyesores on the landscape. Recycling remains an uncommon practice in Czech households, although this is gradually changing as citizens become more educated and willing to improve the quality of their environment.

The Czech government adopted a waste development plan in June 2003. The objective of this plan was to help the Czech Republic work within the framework of EU strategies—in particular, to identify desirable ways to treat and manage waste and find acceptable ways to promote recycling among the Czechs.

THE MINISTRY OF THE ENVIRONMENT

The Czech Republic's commitment to focus more on the environment became evident in 1990 when the Ministry of the Environment of the Czech Republic was established.

Other environmental institutions were formed in the 1990s mainly to support the work of the Ministry of the Environment. These include the Czech Environmental Inspection, responsible for legal enforcement; the State Environmental Fund of the Czech Republic, responsible for acting as a financial instrument of environmental policy; the Central Flood Commission; Eco-Management and Audit Scheme; and the Government Council for Health and the Environment.

The signing of the Aarhus Convention by the Czech Republic in 2004 represented an affirmative step toward the government's commitment to the environment. The Aarhus Convention agrees to provide public access to information, public participation in decision making, and access to justice in environmental matters.

Some Czechs were already active in the environmental movement before the breakup of Czechoslovakia. In fact, many considered the values of wanting a clean, green, and healthy environment as important as their wish for freedom and democracy. Before the Velvet Divorce, the environmental movement was one of the only expressions of protest that was actually permitted by the communist authorities. As a result, many intelligent and talented Czechs used environmentalism as a way of demonstrating their beliefs and worldviews.

There was once only two major environmental nongovernmental organizations (NGOs) in the Czech Republic. They were the Czech Union for Nature Protection and the Brontosaurus Movement. Since January 1990, though, many independent NGOs concerned with environmental issues have been formed. The ones that still exist today work very hard to enhance the environmental health of the Czech Republic. Many of their activities involve education and training, as well as fieldwork. The majority of NGOs feel that they are successful in their environmental labors and make positive contributions to the nation's well-being.

THE FUTURE

The dramatic political changes that have occurred in the Czech Republic since independence have generally had a favorable impact on the environment. Many of the republic's younger generation show an eagerness to learn about all environmental matters and are ready to make the necessary improvements for the good of their new country.

During the years following the fall of communism and the breakup of Czechoslovakia, Czech businesses and the new Czech government tended to focus on creating a strong economy. They had little time or interest for environmental issues. Today, however, as the economy has become more stable and successful, more is being done to tackle environmental issues. There are even incentives in place to encourage good environmental practices in business and industry.

CZECHS

Traditionally dressed girls in Moravia.

CHAPTER 6

BESIDES THE dominant ethnic Czechs, the population is made up of several minority groups. Tensions sometimes erupt between the Czechs and the minority groups over long-standing resentments and issues of racism.

ETHNIC MAKEUP

In a population of approximately 10,220,900, 90 percent are ethnic Czechs, 4 percent are Moravians, 2 percent are Slovak. The other 4 percent are made up of small groups of Poles, Germans, Romanies or Gypsies, and Hungarians. Israelis form a very small but significant minority.

CZECH SELF-IMAGE

On the surface, the Czechs, particularly the older generation, can seem an unfriendly people. On getting to know them better, though, one will find that they are in fact generous and warm people. The younger generation is especially open-minded and eager to meet new people and try new things. Czechs have a reputation for being highly cultured and intellectual with a special interest in the arts and philosophy. Optimism and confidence, however, are not strong Czech traits. This deficit may be linked to their troubled history. The Czechs are similar to their Germanic neighbors—they appear to be serious, responsible, and hardworking. They are often contrasted with the Moravians and Slovaks, who are felt to be more passionate and spontaneous.

Present-day Czechs are the descendants of Slavonic groups that migrated into Central Europe during the fifth and sixth centuries A.D. Those groups inhabited the regions of Bohemia and Moravia as well as western Slovakia, eastern Germany, southern Poland (including Silesia), and northern Hungary.

Today, the Poles have their own Congress of Poles, set up in 1991, which represents Polish interests in the Czech Republic.

GERMANS Germans constitute one of the largest minority groups in the Czech Republic, with a population of approximately 39,000. During World War II there were 3.2 million Germans in Czech lands and Slovakia.

Germanic groups arrived in the region before the Slavs, establishing farming communities around 4000 B.C. Since then, Germans have been a continuous presence in Czech history, often becoming the traditional enemy. Although the Austro-Hungarian Empire was good economically for the Czech lands, culturally it was stifling. The rulers progressively forced German language and culture onto the population until Prague and the other large Czech cities had become essentially German cities. By contrast, the German minority was treated well during the First Republic, between 1918 and 1938. The First Republic was a rich country during those two decades of peace. The Germans had their own schools and even their own university in Prague.

Nazi Germany irrevocably destroyed the social fabric in Czechoslovakia when it took possession of Sudetenland and later occupied the regions of Bohemia and Moravia. The Nazi reign of terror brought swift retaliation against all Germans after World War II, when the Czechs expelled the German minority from Czechoslovakia. Three million Germans were forced out of the country, literally overnight, leaving behind their property and lucrative businesses, especially in the industrial heartland of Bohemia. Those were expropriated by the government. Some 200,000 Germans died in the hardships of the march out of the country—from massacres, exhaustion, and suicide. Resentment and grievances have indelibly stained relations between the two countries. Nevertheless, in Prague on January 21, 1997, the Czech-German Declaration on Mutual Relations and their Future Development was signed—a gesture that won international praise for both nations. The declaration means that both signators agree not to allow political and legal issues from the past affect their present and future relations. Since then, it has been noted that interactions between the two countries have thawed considerably.

GYPSIES Gypsies, or Romanies, are thought to be descendants of migrants from India in the 15th century. The Roma have been treated as inferiors throughout Europe, including the Czech Republic. Before the split into two republics, there were one million Gypsies in Czechoslovakia. Now Gypsies form a group of approximately 12,000 in the Czech Republic, although the true figure is believed to be much higher. Many prefer not to declare their ethnicity as Roma for fear of discrimination.

Gypsy girls enjoying themselves in Brno.

The Gypsy population has sharply increased since the 1950s, both because of births and of migration into Czechoslovakia in search of work, many filling job vacancies left by the Germans who had been forced to leave. The communist government attempted to integrate the Roma into the local society, with limited success. Czechs today are still dismissive of the Gypsies. The mayor of one of Prague's districts was quoted in a newspaper as supporting the idea of moving them out of central districts to the outskirts.

VIETNAMESE The minorities include, interestingly, a small community of Vietnamese who run market stalls and other small businesses. They were employed during the communist era as guest workers to fill gaps in the labor market. Though no longer needed after independence, they refused to return to Vietnam, although they have since faced racism, poor working conditions, and pressure from a government that wants to send them home. Nonetheless, Czechs grudgingly admire the business acumen and work ethic of their Asian guests. There are about 58, 800 Vietnamese (2008 estimate) in the Czech Republic today.

The Jewish Quarter in Prague is known as the Josefov. The first Jewish settlement there was founded in 1091.

ISRAELIS In the 1991 census only 218 people described themselves as Jewish. That number referred specifically to those with Israeli nationality—not people who belonged to the Jewish faith. The number of Jews in the Czech Republic is really much higher. It is, however, but a tiny fraction of the number prior to World War II, when many tens of thousands of Jews from the territory of today's Czech Republic were killed.

OTHERS Nationality figures from the 2001 census show that there are also some smaller minorities, including approximately 20,000 Hungarians, 20,600 Ukrainians, 7,700 Russians, and over 3,000 Greeks and Bulgarians.

A NATION GROWING OLDER

Czechs have become primarily an urban people, with over 70 percent of the population living in the larger towns and cities. Urban congestion has led to smaller living spaces in apartments and a big jump in living expenses, particularly rent. Traditionally, elderly parents live with their adult children when they cannot live alone for health or other reasons, putting further pressure on available space. Contraception and abortion are widely practiced, thus it is not surprising that the rate of population growth is a negative figure: -0.082 percent according to a 2008 estimate. The Czech population is slowly aging.

TRADITIONAL CLOTHING

Folk dress grew in popularity from the 1950s due to the efforts of the communist government to revive patriotism through folkloric traditions—what they called "the people's culture." Folk songs replaced the popular tunes of the day, young people were taught folk dances and discouraged from contemporary dance forms, and May Day processions were replete with traditional dress, flags, and brass bands.

Traditional folk dress is not commonly worn every day in most parts of the republic, but older people in some villages do still wear them, and they always appear at folk festivals. Departing from the simple clothing, usually in drab colors, worn in everyday life, folk garments are embellished with bright, detailed embroidery work.

Czech women display their traditional dress at Prague's Old Town Square.

The abstract or pictorial designs and patterns vary, depending on the season and the age and marital status of the wearer. More elaborate dress evolved for church, weddings, and other special events. The attire also reflects the region—for example, in the eastern parts of the Czech Republic are seen detailed hand-sewn skirts, aprons, and shawls for men and women alike, while in the west one typically sees striking shawls, belts, headgear, and shoes.

These traditional clothes are a disappearing folk practice, barely surviving only through the efforts of minority cultural groups and others whose purpose is to preserve folk culture. Most young people do not willingly participate in folk customs that call for such clothing; it certainly lacks relevance to modern, urban lifestyles. Making these clothes also leads to great expense and effort, prime reasons for abandoning the tradition.

A region near the German border in the northwest is still noted for wearing traditional dress. The inhabitants, called Chods, settled there about a thousand years ago. They are famous for their handicrafts, which include woodcarving and pottery. The residents make an annual pilgrimage to a mountain on the weekend following August 10, where they participate in a festival of bagpipe music and traditional song and dance.

LIFESTYLE

Strollers enjoying the scene on the streets of Karlovy Vary.

CHAPTER 7

Since the fall of communism, the Czech way of life has changed rapidly. Most Czechs live in the country's larger towns and in the cities. The family is very important in Czech society, and bonds remain strong even after marriage. The Czech Republic has high literacy rates due to its compulsory education for youth aged 6 to 16.

THE OVERTHROW OF COMMUNISM in 1989 influenced many aspects of Czech work and social life. Initially people were reluctant to forego some of the privileges that communism once had afforded them, such as a more relaxed work routine. There was also disappointment that instant wealth for all did not follow the introduction of capitalism. There was widespread pessimism over the rising cost of living paired with inadequate income. Today, however, a measure of realism has seeped into the Czech way of life, and working people no longer expect capitalism to bestow riches upon them.

TRANSITION TO DEMOCRACY AND CAPITALISM

The demise of communism and the rapid move into a democratic, free enterprise society, along with separation from Slovakia, have brought about many changes that have altered people's lives. Czechs now are growing accustomed to a more capitalistic way of life.

The Art Nouveau facade of the Grand Hotel Europa in Prague is a beautiful example of the stunning architecture that can be found in the Czech Republic.

CITY LIVING For most Czechs, Prague is the ultimate in city living. The Czech appetite for going out and socializing is whetted by the vast number of cafés, pubs, and restaurants to be visited. It is not just about going out for a bite, however. Prague buildings display an amazing array of architectural styles and decor, which makes dining out a special occasion. The Grand Hotel Europa, built in 1889 and then subsequently rebuilt between 1904 and 1905, is one example. The café at ground level is crowned by an oval gallery, and polished timbers gleam throughout. Here people can sit and warm their hands on a cup of delicious hot chocolate and watch others going about their business outside on the busy street in Wenceslas Square.

Prague is one of the few cities in Europe that was not bombed during World War II, consequently, it still has many beautiful old buildings. There are houses in Prague dating back to at least the early 18th century. Above their front doors are signs or ornamental frames made of metal, stone, or wood. These cartouches, as they are commonly called, indicated the original occupant's social rank or profession and helped to identify the building. Street numbers were introduced in 1770. Today, many Czechs continue to live in such houses, sometimes inhabiting an ancestral home that has belonged to the family for centuries. Descendants of the world-renowned Art Nouveau artist Alphonse Mucha continue to live in the house he inhabited when he returned from Paris in 1910. Above the first-floor windows and directly above the main entrance is a large cartouche elaborately outlined in curls and contours.

RURAL LIVING In old farmhouses, whether they are one-bedroom shacks or two-story buildings, activities are centered around the stove. Often there is a built-in bench right next to the stove for the little tasks that can be done while keeping warm, like darning socks or fixing a broken harness. Typically, the area around the stove is covered in strikingly colored ceramic tiles. Near the stove and along the wall hang enamel pots. If the house has a second story, the main bedroom is located directly above the stove in order to take advantage of its rising warmth.

Rural holiday homes are often constructed of wood.

Many country dwellings are constructed of wood. The surface of a wall is often decorated with strips of wood arranged in patterns, providing texture and interest. Window frames have elaborate designs. Individual preferences for ornamentation is also shown in wardrobes, chests of drawers, and other furniture, which are typically painted with elaborate patterns, both abstract and figurative. Hand-embroidered bedcovers contrast beautifully with the dark tones of the wooden head- and footboards. Czechs enjoy the simple pleasures of their country homes, especially as weekend or vacation retreats. They deeply appreciate the stillness and beauty of the countryside.

THE FAMILY

A nuclear family of parents and their children is the basic Czech family unit, while the bond between extended family members is generally lifelong, too. Although people, particularly the younger generation, relocate more often than in the past for work reasons, contact between siblings after marriage remains constant.

In many families, *babička* (BAB-ich-ka), or the grandmother, is the key figure. Grandmothers enjoy much respect as a source of wisdom, but they also are figures of authority. They often serve as babysitters, or live with the young parents, as it is common for both parents to work. The legendary status of the grandmother is described in the 1855 novel *Babička*, by Božena Němcová, which is an all-time favorite with Czechs of all ages.

Strong Czech women working in the fields. Women make up a large proportion of the country's labor force and are essential breadwinners in most families.

THE ROLE OF WOMEN

Eighty-eight percent of Czech women of productive age work full time. Women constitute 47 percent of the total labor force, with 12.5 percent of women considering themselves the sole and 48 percent the partial breadwinners for their families. The discussion of women's rights really surfaced in Czech society only after 1989. The first public debate on feminism was broadcast on television in 1992, and a single book that was hailed as the first Czech feminist writing was published that year, too.

Part of the reason that feminism has not been evident in the Czech Republic may be the legacy of socialist policies. Under the communist regime, women's entitlements already included equal pay for equal work, equal educational opportunities, and six months' maternity leave at full pay. Nurseries and kindergartens were provided in local communities and in the workplace. Public institutions employed a greater number of women than in the West because of gender quotas set by the government.

Detractors of communist ideology argue that socialism actually exploited women. By placing women in the workforce, many Czech families became accustomed to having two incomes, instead of just one. Women, however, were expected to continue to shoulder the traditional responsibilities of home and children. Despite the law on equal pay, 45 percent of women surveyed in 1991 reported their pay to be less than that of men for the same kind of work, and women were more likely to be fired. In 2005, the average wage for women in the Czech Republic was 73 percent of men's wage level. Czechs do not appear to challenge certain premises that influence and restrict any trend toward real gender equality. They see gender differences as embedded in nature, resulting directly from the biological differences between men and women. Many women emphasize their unique experience of childbearing, and both men and women argue that most women's desires are almost entirely focused on the bearing and raising of children.

Many Czech women consider themselves strong and individualistic. Their communist heritage has encouraged them to believe that they can explore any field of study and choose any profession they please. Czech women today are primarily concerned with greater representation in politics, so that they themselves can address issues such as education, child benefits, child care, maternity benefits, and other family policy and family law issues. Many women also believe that the presence of women in parliament would lead to more compassionate and honest government.

Most Czech women prefer not to call themselves feminists. Unlike many of their counterparts in the west, Czech women see women's rights as a natural part of all human rights. Many Czech women are practical and continue to assert themselves by gaining access to higher education and professional employment. There is a growing number of Czech women who are active in business and political life.

WEDDINGS

Czechs tend to marry young, especially in rural areas. A girl unmarried at 22 may be thought of as "on the shelf." Traditionally, girls were pressured to "catch" a man before he went off to complete his military service, but such pressures are declining and compulsory military service no longer applies. Folk customs are still part of village weddings. Elaborately embroidered clothes are worn, special songs and dances performed, and old rituals such as the mock abduction of the bride are also reenacted.

A grammar school in Koeniggraetz, Hradec Kralove. School attendance is compulsory for all Czechs up to the age of 16.

A LITERATE PEOPLE

Education in primary and secondary schools, from ages 6 to 16, is compulsory, and continues to be fully funded by the state. There are also state kindergartens for children aged 3 to 6 and secondary schools preparing students aged 15 to 18 for university. The literacy rate is around 99 percent, with 97 percent of Czechs progressing to secondary education and 30 percent enrolled in tertiary education. Czechs consider themselves to be educated people. They revere education and encourage their children to do well academically. The republic has many universities and other institutes of higher learning. The main ones are the Charles University and the Czech Technical University in Prague, the Masaryk University in Brno, the Palacký University in Olomouc and the Liberec University of Technology.

Expenditure on education is 4.4 percent of GDP and the average school-life expectancy from primary through tertiary education is 15 years for both male and female students. The number of graduates has increased from approximately 30,000 in 2000 to 63,000 in 2007. The most popular fields of study are medicine, economics, teaching, and social work.

THE HEALTH CRISIS

Czech health service has undergone drastic transformation after the political changes in 1989. The national health system was dismantled and freedom of choice of health care was adopted in 1990 and 1991. Major reforms have included the decentralization and liberalization of the health care system.

In 1992 a compulsory health insurance system was introduced, based on individual contributions. Those are paid by individuals and by employers or by the state. Czechs pay 13.5 percent of their income before taxes to the private insurance companies that collect such premiums. Currently, employers contribute 9 percent for health insurance on behalf of each employee.

Foreigners who require medical services in any hospital or clinic have to pay for their own treatment. Many doctors and medical staffers, particularly in Prague, speak English. When treating foreigners, doctors, hospitals, and even ambulance services often expect immediate cash or credit card payments for their services.

Unfortunately, the Czech health care system continues to be beset with problems, including financial deficits as well as a lack of regulation and enabling legislation.

WORKING LIFE

As in many other European countries, the workday for most employees usually begins at 8 A.M. and ends between 4 and 5 P.M. Most banks are open from 8 A.M. to 6 P.M. Banks and most offices are open Monday through Friday. Stores tend to be open from 8 or 9 A.M. to 5 or 6 P.M., including Saturday. Some shops open later, and some supermarkets are open for 24 hours. In larger towns and cities, you can now find many other stores that are open for 24 hours, sometimes seven days a week. Smaller shops may close for lunch between the hours of 12 noon and 2 P.M. Most businesses close on Sundays, apart from restaurants, cafés, bars, movie theaters, and shopping centers.

When Czechs die, they are often escorted to their final resting place by amateur woodwind bands, usually made up of members of the local fire brigade.

RELIGION

Saint Nicholas Church at Malostranske Namesto in Prague.

CHAPTER 8

The numerous churches and cathedrals that dot the Czech Republic's landscape are testament to the country's religious past. However, the oppression that the communist regime brought with it has turned many Czechs away from any sort of religious beliefs, to the extent that many of them profess to be atheist.

SINCE THE INTRODUCTION OF Christianity to the Czech lands in the ninth century, Czech worshipers have swung from Catholicism to Protestantism and then back to Catholicism. Under the communist regime (1948—89), people were banned from expressing religious beliefs at all. Their history has strongly determined the strength of Czechs' religious beliefs today and the role religion plays in their lives.

THE CHRISTIAN EMISSARIES

The Greek monks Cyril and Methodius, who were brothers, brought Christianity to the Czech lands in A.D. 863. Their work in Central and Eastern Europe involved translating the Bible into the various local spoken languages. Cyril, the younger of the two, was educated at a school for children of the Byzantine imperial family. He had a gift for languages and held prestigious positions as professor of philosophy at the Magnaura Palace School and as librarian of Saint Sofia Cathedral in Constantinople (modern Istanbul). The Greek missionary brothers belonged to the Orthodox Christian Church of Constantinople. In the Czech area they translated the Bible into the Slavic language of the time, causing much controversy because it was seen as heretical to teach Christianity in any language other than one of the then holy languages—

Tyn Church in Prague's Old Town Square was the Hussite's place of worship before they were defeated by the Catholics in 1620.

as they are considered irrelevant to daily life. Despite their reduced congregations, churches in larger cities are still crowded because of the many tourists interested in them.

There appears to be a reluctance among Czechs to be expressive Christians. Some Czechs have warned of the danger of the Catholic Church becoming authoritarian and hence undemocratic.

The Catholic Church has been compensated by the government for church property the communist government had confiscated in the past. Part of those funds has gone toward restoring and maintaining Catholic churches throughout the country. There are now many beautiful old churches in the countryside as well as in the cities.

The Protestants are represented by several groups in the Czech Republic, the largest being the Hussite Church, which has retained the doctrine of the double communion—both bread and wine. Other Protestant denominations include the Evangelical Church of Czech Brethren.

Although many Czechs are not devout Christians in practice, Czechs in general believe in a moral upbringing for their children that will guide them into responsible citizenship with a civic sense of duty. The notion of a civil society is close to the heart of most Czechs. They revere their first president, Tomáš Garrigue Masaryk, for his philosophical background and his ardent support of democracy and tolerance.

CZECH JUDAISM

The presence of Jews in the Czech lands began in the 11th century, and grew to their having thriving communities and businesses in Prague. In the 13th century, however, the Roman Catholic Church decreed that Jews

The Jubilee Synagogue in Prague was built in Art Nouveau and Pseudo Moorish styles.

and Christians should live separately. The Jews were crowded into a walled ghetto. Jews in the Czech lands have been alternately welcomed and persecuted for several centuries—welcomed, because they were successful traders and craftsmen and paid lucrative taxes, yet persecuted by mobs and rulers alike and forced to defend their synagogues and private property from sanctioned plunder. Under Empress Maria Theresa (1740–70), Jews were exiled from Prague and forced to pay special taxes. Her son, Emperor Joseph II (1780–90), decreed religious tolerance, but it was because he needed more money from able taxpayers. He ordered the ghetto walls torn down, and the Jewish quarter was made a borough of Prague. It was named Josefov in his honor.

Czech Jews who survived World War II sorrowfully remember another ghetto, Theresienstadt (modern Terezín), which was created by the Germans

An aerial view of the Josefov quarter of Prague as it is today.

as a "distribution camp" to sort the trainloads of Jews before passing them on to concentration camps. From Prague alone, 40,000 Jews made their final journey to this ghetto. Anti-Semitism was a characteristic of the communist regime also, although it was not as lethal as that promoted by Hitler. Unfortunately, anti-Semitism continues in the Czech Republic today.

Only 6,000 Jews remain in the Czech Republic today. The largest Jewish community, of 4,000, continues to be located in the Josefov quarter of Prague. There are smaller communities in Brno and Ostrava.

In 1997 Czech leaders finally agreed to compensate Slovak Jews for gold and other valuables that the fascist regime had confiscated from Slovak Holocaust victims in World War II. The valuables had been deposited in the Czechoslovak State Bank in 1953 and assimilated into the federal budget. Approximately $590,000 was paid into a foundation run by Jewish organizations. The Czech government paid two-thirds of the total and the Slovak government the rest.

PLACES OF WORSHIP

The long history of Christianity and Judaism in the Czech Republic has resulted in the erection of beautiful and architecturally significant places

SUPERSTITIONS

Czechs, especially those who live in the countryside, are superstitious folks. Grandparents will spellbind children with frightening tales that usually convey some moral precept or warning. One example is the story of the waterman. In the Czech Republic there are many ponds, and the legends recount that a waterman lives in each. He is a terrifying figure. When young girls go to his pond to wash their clothes, he springs out of the water, snatches them, and pulls them down to his lair. In his underwater world the waterman has little pots in which he keeps the souls of the children he captures.

of worship. Prague boasts some of the best known among them, including Saint Vitus Cathedral. Located in the heart of Hradčany, the cathedral's foundation stone was laid in 1344 by Charles IV, but the cathedral was not completed until 1929, when a concerted effort was made to finish the work during the Czech National Revival Movement. Consequently, it is a mixture of Gothic, Renaissance, and Baroque styles. The doorways are richly decorated with carvings of historical and biblical scenes, and the interior is illuminated by traditional and modern stained glass windows. Unfortunately, it is among Prague's many stately and important buildings in dire need of renovation and cleaning to rid its blackened surface of the effects of aging and pollution.

In Josefov, half a dozen original synagogues remain standing. The Old-New Synagogue is Europe's oldest synagogue. The main part was built in 1270, and women's prayer galleries were added in the 17th century. Some features of the synagogue that resembled symbols of Christian churches have been destroyed. Other synagogues in Josefov have been refitted into museums to exhibit sacred Jewish artifacts, many of which were rescued from demolished Bohemian synagogues. Such beloved places dedicated to their culture and religion are of great significance to Jews of the Czech Republic and others everywhere. Ironically, they were spared by Hitler from destruction so that they might be used as part of his "museum of an extinct race."

LANGUAGE

Floor-to-ceiling shelves of books line the walls of Philosophical Hall in the Strahov Library at Strahov Monastery in Prague.

CHAPTER 9

LANGUAGE CANNOT BE SEPARATED from notions of culture, civilization, and identity. Czechs are proud of their language, which they have had to defend against foreign rulers. They see themselves as cultured and educated people, and the fastidious way they use their language reflects those attributions.

A LANGUAGE IN THE MAKING

Most modern European, Middle Eastern, and Indian languages are derived from the family of languages called Indo-European. Czech belongs to one branch of the group, Common Slavonic.

The Slavic groups that settled in the Czech lands had evolved a common language as early as the ninth century. In A.D. 863, two Byzantine monks, the brothers Cyril and Methodius, translated the Bible into the Czech local language and thus a written form of Slavonic was produced for the first time.

In the Middle Ages, Old Church Slavonic was replaced by Latin, the language of medieval European learning. That was followed by the consolidation of German in the Bohemian kingdom, as many rulers of that period were German. The establishment of Charles University in Prague in 1348, by the Czech king and Holy Roman emperor Charles IV, fostered the development of the Czech language. It was the first university to be built in Central Europe.

Words are often borrowed from one language and absorbed into another. Polka, pistol, and robot are Czech words that have settled comfortably into the English language. "Robot," derived from the Czech word *robotnik* (serf), was coined by Czech novelist, playwright, and essayist Karel Čapek in his play, *Rossum's Universal Robots*, in 1921, to describe a machine-made man, an automaton.

Road signs in the Czech language.

Czech and Slovak are closely related linguistically. The older generation of Czechs and Slovaks can easily understand each other. This is not the case, however, among the younger generation who have not been as exposed to each other's language.

After their defeat in the Thirty Years' War (1618—48), Czechs were once again dominated by a foreign civilization. They lost their rights as citizens, and German replaced the Czech language in the public affairs of the region. Czech culture and literature were stifled, but the spoken language survived in the countryside, where peasants continued to use their own language. This led to a social barrier between the lower and rural classes on one side and the noble and urban classes on the other.

In the 19th century, Josef Dobrovský (1753—1829), a Jesuit priest and scholar, wrote a systematic grammar of the Czech language. Later, František Palacký (1798—1876), a historian and politician, published a history of Bohemia, a work in five volumes written between 1836 and 1867. Both writers were important in establishing Czech lands and language amid the European community of nations.

In the late 19th century, nationalistic sentiments took off across the continent, and language became a crucial issue. Recognizing the need to assert their own cultural heritage, Czechs demanded the freedom to speak and

FOREIGN INFLUENCES

It is inevitable that the German language continues to play a role in the Czech Republic, especially as the nation shares a border with Germany. Germanisms are present in the border dialects and in colloquial language. In the past, young male Czechs would travel to German-speaking areas in search of apprenticeships, returning fluent in German, while girls often went into domestic service in German-speaking Austrian households. Despite racial tensions, Germans and Austrians remain Czechs' closest contact with the Western world. It is therefore expedient for Czechs, especially those in the service industries, to speak German, and Germans are widely sought as customers and business partners.

Since the Velvet Revolution of 1989, foreign investment has been encouraged by the Czech government. There was also a widespread acknowledgement that Czechs needed foreigners to join their companies to teach local workers new skills and impart knowledge. As a result, the English language has also established a foothold in the country, primarily in the major cities, in the areas of tourism and business. Many expatriate Britons, Americans, and Irish working in the cities are active in the republic's campaign to replace Russian with English as the foreign language of choice, and language schools eagerly employ native English speakers. The campaign has been successful, and language schools offering English continue to thrive.

This situation may have reached a plateau in the business world, where private companies are employing fewer foreign workers as more Czechs workers have been brought up-to-date. Many help-wanted ads in major newspapers, especially in Prague, however, continue to request bilingual Czech/English speakers. Czechs have quickly come to realize the prominence of the English language in the rest of Europe. Because they were forced to learn Russian at school under the communist regime as their first foreign language, many Czechs can still speak Russian but choose not to.

write in their own language. They succeeded in 1918, when the independent Republic of Czechoslovakia was formed. Since then, the Czech language has not faced any real threat except during World War II, when the Nazis shut down institutions of learning. Later, under the communists, learning Russian as a second language was made compulsory in schools.

A bookstore in the Czech Republic. About 99 percent of the country's population is literate.

CZECH IN THE MODERN WORLD

The modern Czech language is spoken by over 10 million people. It is written in the roman script, as is English. Above some vowels and consonants are accent marks that determine pronunciation.

Czech is a complex language where nouns are divided according to gender; for example, table in Czech is masculine, book is feminine, and bicycle is neuter. It is also a highly inflected language, that is to say that the word meanings subtly change according to usage, conjugation, and pronunciation. The ending of a noun depends on what role the noun plays in the sentence (is it the subject doing an action, or the object?), while the ending of a verb depends on its tense: present, past, or future.

Friends stop for a chat in Telc's Old Town Square. Bicycling is a popular way of getting around.

FORMS OF ADDRESS

As every noun in Czech has a gender, surnames differ depending on whether they are male or female. The wife of a man whose surname is Navrátil would be known as Navrátilová. Czechs address one another with the honorary titles of *Pan* (PAHN, Mister), *Paní* (PA-ni, Missus), and *Slečna* (SLE-tchna, Miss). Titles such as doctor and professor for teachers are also used. Forms of address combine the primary form (*Pan*, *Paní*, *Slečna*), with other titles, for example, "*Pan Doctor* Navratil."

GREETINGS

Shaking hands is customary upon meeting someone. Even people in a hurry will reach out to clasp each other's hands momentarily. Close friends also exchange kisses on both cheeks, men and women alike.

A Moravian churchman and educator, Jan Amos Comenius (1592–1670), favored learning Latin to facilitate the study of European culture. He believed in using the spoken language and encouraged learning languages through conversation. He strove for a system of education with equal opportunity for all, including women. He is seen as a true pioneer of education.

ARTS

An artist patiently paints an Easter egg with an intricate design.

CHAPTER 10

The arts of the Czech Republic are visible and audible throughout the country. Its rich history is reflected in its architecture, and every street musician is testament to the nation's passion for music.

THE CZECHS HAVE EXPRESSED A strong affinity for the arts throughout their entire history. Their buildings are magnificent examples of Gothic, Renaissance, and Baroque styles; Czech composers, writers, dramatists, and craftsmen have enriched the world stage; and literary and musical festivals are esteemed annual events.

THE EVOLUTION OF DRAMA

Czech drama goes back to pre-Christian times when festivals included theatrical performances; they are still a part of the rural scene. In the 13th century, plays performed in the Czech language had themes taken from daily life. By the 16th century Czech-language theater had established itself, and its themes were mainly biblical. At Charles University in Prague, plays were performed in Latin and were used as a method of teaching. Some plays, known as *schola ludus*, or school games, were written by the renowned educator Jan Amos Comenius in the 17th century. After the Thirty Years' War, the Czech-language theater vanished, reappearing only more than a century later, in Prague.

Right: Children in traditional Moravian costumes dance in a theatrical production.

The First Czechoslovak Republic supported much experimentation in theater. In contrast, the communist period after World War II welcomed the production of good classical theater, but hardly any modern productions. Plays produced by dissident playwrights such as Václav Havel—later to be elected president—were banned because of their antigovernment bias. The Western world gained access to them, though, so the work of the dissidents became known outside their own country. The mid- to late 1960s provided a respite from government censorship, and consequently, free expression was explored in Prague's theaters, such as the Theater by the Railings, which was founded in 1958.

Since the overthrow of communism, new theater groups have flowered. The Czech Republic plays host to an annual international theater festival, which draws enthusiastic crowds. Theatergoing is a passion for many Czechs, especially the elderly.

PUPPET THEATER Marionette plays have been popular since the 16th century, their demand peaking in the 17th and early 18th centuries. They were considered children's entertainment until a revival in the 20th century. Josef Skupa's legendary puppets, Spejbl and Hurvínek, created in the 1920s, still perform in Prague.

Traditional marionettes for sale in Prague. Puppet theater is popular in the Czech Republic.

Street musicians performing in Prague. Many Czechs are musically proficient and join local groups.

NATURALLY MUSICAL

Czechs have a common saying: "Scratch a Czech, find a musician underneath." The Arab explorer Ibrahim ibn Jakub described string and woodwind instruments used by the Slavs in the region of Bohemia in A.D. 965. A rare 11th- or 12th-century lute is the earliest intact instrument found in that region. Four 14th century hymns in the Czech language have also been discovered.

The 15th-century Hussite Movement (named after religious reformer Jan Hus) was responsible for the creation of distinctive Czech hymns. Folk music developed swiftly after that and is still enjoyed in villages today. That early spurt was followed by a period of stagnation when Czech music survived only at the village level, or was kept alive by Czech emigrants, such as the composer Jan Dismas Zelenka, who worked in Dresden in the 18th century.

The 19th century was a rich and productive time. Bedřich Smetana (1824–84), believed to be the first nationalist Czech composer, departed from traditional melodies in composing his operas and symphonic poems.

Violin maker Josef Kantuscher lovingly works on a violin.

beginnings of a group of skilled workers who were to become Czech masters appeared in a small town called Passkey, in the hills dividing northern Bohemia from German Silesia. Věnceslav Metelka, a joiner and self-taught violin maker, trained his sons and daughter in the trade. A school established itself there over time, with more family members becoming artisans and taking on pupils. The Metelka family is but one example of the long-standing traditions of musical artisanship that became embedded in the national psyche. The Czechs can rightly claim that musical prowess runs in their veins.

The violins made in these traditional shops varied in shape and curve, the type of woods used, the size and angles of the holes, the quality of the acoustics, and even the color and formulas of the wood varnish. Many violin makers placed labels with their names on their products, although often the name of the shop owner rather than the apprentice would appear on the finished instrument. Many of those men were musicians as well, and had a deep affinity with their craft. At about this time, too, the working class began to develop an interest in cultural pursuits, and many locally made violins found their way into middle-class homes.

FOLK ARTS AND CRAFTS

Much of the physical evidence of Czech folk traditions reaches back only to the 19th-century National Revival Movement, because of the perishable nature of most materials, such as wood and clay. Folk arts take the forms of stories, songs, music, dance, clothing, and architectural styles. Those traditions have been preserved to this day in families, passing from each generation to a younger one, or publicly, through museums and festivals.

Folk festivals usually occur in the summer or fall. They provide occasions for neighbors to gather and enjoy themselves with music and dancing and the wearing of traditional folk dress. The sleepy town of Strážnice (STRAJ-nitse), for example, suddenly springs to life at the end of June for the International Folklore Festival. Participants from all over Europe take part in spirited competitions.

Czechs dressed in traditional Chod clothing during a folk festivals.

FOLK MUSEUMS All over the countryside are open-air museums called *skansens* (SKAN-suhn) that incorporate traditional architecture and furnishings. Some are sites of folk festivals, and the better ones attempt to show not only single buildings but also the way entire communities lived. For that purpose, barns, churches, homes, and other buildings have been transported piece by piece and filled with utensils, linen, furniture, and clothing typical of the period.

BOHEMIAN CRYSTAL

A legend tells of an old woman walking through the Giant Mountains carrying a basket of newly made glassware to market. She slipped and fell, smashing her goods to pieces. Devastated though she was, she listened to Krakonoš, the spirit of the mountains, who commanded her to take her basket of shattered glass home. Upon her arrival, she found that the broken glass had been transformed into gold!

Czechs, especially Bohemians, have been discovering gold in the trade of cut and engraved glass and crystal for several centuries. In the second half of the 17th century, the small trade of glass cutting and engraving formally

A glassmaker at work at a crystal factory in Prague.

established itself into guilds. As interest in decorated glass grew, Bohemian craftsmen developed a rock crystal type of glass, which expanded the range of possible decoration. Limestone was the key ingredient in this glass, giving it greater brilliance and providing a still more striking contrast against the matte engraving.

By the end of the 17th century, the knowledge of how to make limestone crystal glass had spread throughout Bohemia and reached other parts of Europe. Bohemian glass began to be exported, and by the end of the 18th century was known in most of Europe, the Middle East, and the Americas. Engravers found inspiration in many sources—biblical tales, images on coins and maps, and the landscape around them. Bohemian artisans also traveled widely with their wares and customized their products to buyers' requests.

Glass and crystal continue to be produced in Bohemia today. As with most crafts that began before the industrial revolution, glass cutting and engraving have grown into an industry based on mass production. The days when only the nobility were able to afford such beautiful objects are gone. Engraved glass and crystal are now affordable commodities.

LITERATURE

The earliest Czech literary works were hymns and religious texts in Old Church Slavonic and 10th-century legends of Saint Wenceslas. Jan Hus's *Orthographia Bohemica* was among the religious tracts of the 14th century. Themes of morality and chronicles of daily life and of journeys were featured in 16th- and 17th-century prose. The persecution of secular scholars since the 17th century discouraged local creative writing for about two centuries.

BETWEEN BLACK AND WHITE

In the 20th century, photography as an art form took root in the Czech lands. One artist in this field was Josef Sudek (1896–1976), who was apprenticed at the age of 15 to a bookbinder. A fellow worker introduced him to amateur photography, and after losing his right arm fighting in World War I, he decided to become a photographer. He studied photography at the School of Graphic Art in Prague for two years. Sudek absorbed influences from past and contemporary painting traditions, and in time he came to express a unique, romantic style, concentrating on gradations of tone between black and white. One of his most striking series is of Saint Vitus Cathedral in Prague, which was undergoing renovation—over 100 photographs juxtaposing the grand cathedral with the ordinary details of building materials. Sudek dedicated himself to photographing his country, especially Prague. Many exhibitions of his work were held during his lifetime, in his country and abroad, notably in New York City. In his later years he worked commercially just enough to earn money for his living expenses, preferring to concentrate on his creative visions. He said, "You should never lose contact with that which is close to your heart; at the most you can make an interruption for half a year. If it is longer, you lose the thread and never find it again."

From the mid-19th to the early 20th centuries, Czech writers developed nationalistic and political themes. Among the writers of that period are Jaroslav Hašek (1883–1923) and Karel Čapek (1890–1938). Hašek, a practical joker, had a colorful career—he was, in turn, bank clerk, newspaper editor (by age 21), soldier in World War I, prisoner of war of the Russians, and communist propagandist for the Bolsheviks before turning to writing full time. Best known for *The Good Soldier* (Švejk), a satire on military life, Hašek's novels made fun of authoritarian regimes. Čapek, a Czech novelist, playwright, and essayist, explored morality in his works. He often collaborated with his brother Josef, a dramatist and illustrator, in writing plays.

Early in the same period, Jan Neruda (1834–91) wrote popular light fiction about 19th-century Prague. Two famous collections of his are *Tales of the Lesser Quarter* and *Pictures of Old Prague*.

Jewish writer Franz Kafka was one of the Czech Republic's most influential authors.

There used to be a strong Czech tradition of writing in German. An influential Austrian group known as the Prague Circle included Jewish fiction writer Franz Kafka (1883—1924), novelist, poet, and playwright Franz Werfel (1890—1945), and the poet Rainer Maria Rilke (1875—1926). When World War II ended, the German minority was expelled, and that linguistic tradition ended abruptly.

Communism dampened the literary spirit; the 1950s turned out writing in the socialist realist style. Nevertheless, the Prague Spring of the 1960s saw a flowering of writing with authors such as Milan Kundera. After the invasion of Warsaw Pact troops in 1968, Kundera was among the writers who were forced to leave the country in order to continue their work.

POETIC TENDENCIES Czech poetry is not popularly read in other countries because it is difficult to translate and interpret. Karel Hynek Mácha (1810—36) is considered the greatest 19th-century Czech poet. He was greatly influenced by English and Polish Romantic literature, and his lyrical epic *Máj* (*May*) has been highly praised by 20th-century poets and critics. Mácha tragically died of pneumonia just before his 26th birthday.

Jaroslav Seifert (1901—86) was a journalist until 1950, then a freelance writer. His poetry reflects the momentous events of the German occupation of Czechoslovakia, the Soviet coup of 1948, and the liberation of the Prague Spring. His poetry and articles lost publishers because of his opposition to the Soviet invasion. His themes ranged from patriotism to political critiques. His work began to be republished in the Czech Republic in 1979. Jaroslav Seifert won the Nobel Prize in Literature in 1984.

PAINTING

Early examples of painting in the Czech lands include illuminated manuscripts and church frescoes of the Romanesque period and Byzantine paintings in the late 13th century. Book illumination was the dominant form of painting during the late Gothic and Renaissance periods.

MILAN KUNDERA

Milan Kundera was born on April 1, 1929, in Brno. He studied filmmaking at the Academy of Music and Dramatic Arts in Prague (FAMU) and focused on writing films and directing. In 1954 he became a lecturer in literature at FAMU where he taught until 1969. Meanwhile, he gained prominence for his work in poetry, drama, film, prose, and fiction. His first novel, The Joke, *and a collection of stories,* Laughable Loves, *were published in Prague before 1968.* The Joke *was translated into more than 20 languages and brought him international recognition. After the Warsaw Pact invasion of Czechoslovakia, Kundera was marked as a dissident by the communist government. He moved to France where he taught comparative literature. In 1979, in reaction to the publication of his novel* The Book of Laughter and Forgetting, *the Czechoslovak government revoked his Czech citizenship. Two years later he became a naturalized French citizen.*

Kundera's literary awards include the Czechoslovak Writers Publishing House Prize for his critical study of novelist Vladislav Vančura in Art of the Novel *(1961) and for* Laughable Loves *(1969); the Klement Lukeš Prize (1963) for his play* The Owners of the Keys; *the Czechoslovak Writers Union Prize (1968) for* The Joke; *the French Prix Médicis (1973) for* Life Is Elsewhere; *the Italian Premio Letterario Mondello (1978) for* The Farewell Waltz; *the American Commonwealth Award and the Prix Europa-Littérature in recognition of his contribution to literature; and the Los Angeles Times Prize in 1984 for* The Unbearable Lightness of Being, *which was made into a motion picture. In 1985 Milan Kundera received the Jerusalem Prize, awarded every two years to "the writer who has contributed most to the world's understanding of the freedom of the individual in society." But Czechs are stubbornly ambivalent toward Kundera, feeling that he is no longer "Czech" as he now writes in French and does not allow his French texts to be translated into Czech.*

The Old Town and castle in Český Krumlov was built in the 13th century and was reworked in the 16th-century Renaissance style.

Czech realism flowered during the later stages of the revival movement in the 19th century when subject matters dealt mostly with the prosaic. An era of landscape art was followed by Impressionism and Symbolism.

Art Nouveau became very popular in the late 19th and early 20th centuries. Many Czech artists were inspired by the Art Nouveau styles of Paris. Among them was Alphonse Mucha (1860–1939), famed for his delicate female figures whose hair and clothing merged with the background in elaborate, decorative detail. He achieved fame for his posters advertising French actress Sarah Bernhardt in her many roles. In his later travels to the United States, he met Chicago industrialist Charles Richard Crane, who sponsored 20 large historical paintings in the series Epic of the Slavic People, which were painted between 1912 and 1930.

Surrealism inspired Czech artists in the early 20th century and continues to be an influential mode with painters. For artists such as Eva Švankmajerová, the focus of surrealism is the freedom of the individual, still highly relevant.

ARCHITECTURE

The earliest buildings in Bohemia and Moravia were made of wood. The oldest surviving buildings were built in the Romanesque style with thick walls, rounded arches, and large, closely spaced columns. From the 13th to 16th centuries, the Gothic style dominated public architecture in the Czech lands. Individual buildings, as well as town squares surrounded by arcaded houses built in that period, are still in use today.

In the early 16th century, the Italian Renaissance style developed distinct Czech touches, including stucco decorations of historical scenes. Good examples of the Baroque style of the early 18th century can be seen throughout the country. Its distinctive features include grand sculptures and frescoes, and gilded ornamentation. In the 19th century there was a revival of prior architectural styles—neoclassical, neo-Gothic, and neo-Renaissance. Many beautiful hotels and cafés in Prague evoke that period. The communist era trampled creativity, leaving a legacy of ugly, massive, concrete public buildings and villages thrown together with prefabricated housing.

Many standing architectural treasures, however, are in need of restoration, and the government has set aside funds for their conservation. One of the more well-known modern Czech architects is Bořek Šípek. Born in Prague in 1949, he is the architect of Prague Castle under the presidency of Václav Havel.

MOVIES

The Czech film industry in the early 20th century turned out mainly silent comedies. The Nazi occupiers restricted film production to nationalistic comedies, and the communist regime that followed allowed only low-quality propaganda films. The number of films made after World War II declined. Nonetheless, Karel Steklý's *Siren* (1947) was awarded the Golden Lion in Venice. Twelve-year-old Ivan Jandl was the first Czech awarded an Oscar, for a role in *The Search*, a 1948 film by Fred Zinnemann that starred Montgomery Clift. Other major Czech films include *The Shop on Main Street* (*Obchod na korze*, 1965) and Jiří Menzel's *Closely Watched Trains* (*Ostře sledované vlaky*, 1966) which won Oscars for Best Foreign Language Film in the 1960s. Among the nominated movies for an Oscar were also *My Sweet Little Village* (*Vesničko má středisková*) in 1986, *The Elementary School* (*Obecná škola*) in 1991, *Divided We Fall* (*Musíme si pomáhat*) in 2000, and *Želary* in 2003.

Despite tense political conditions in the 1950s, Czech films attained some success abroad. In 1958 Karel Zeman's *The Invention of Destruction* was awarded the Expo 58 Grand Prix in Brussels and Jiri Weiss's *The Wolf Trap* won the International Federation of Film Critics Award in Venice.

Young Czech directors escaped censorship because, as the first graduates of the Academy of Film under communist rule, they were assumed to be ideologically clean slates. The director Miloš Forman began his career during this period but fled to the United States after the Warsaw Pact invasion in 1968. He is well-known for *One Flew Over the Cuckoo's Nest* and *Amadeus*. Czech cinema's greatest success in recent years was the 1996 movie *Kolya*, directed by Jan Svěrák, that won an Oscar for Best Foreign Film.

LEISURE

Children enjoy a day at the playground.

CHAPTER 11

CZECHS PURSUE A number of activities for their enjoyment, from traditional sports and games to pastimes such as gathering mushrooms and berry picking or simply spending weekends at their country cottage, often gardening there.

Czechs enjoy sports and theater in their free time. Many of them are also avid travelers, taking trips abroad or to their vacation country homes or to a spa resort.

THE SOKOL MOVEMENT

Physical education has a long tradition in the republic. A Czech professor of art history at Charles University, Miroslav Tyrs (1832—84), founded an exercise movement called Sokol in 1862. He was convinced that citizens needed to be of healthy mind and body in order to survive as a nation. Although the movement was based on a tradition of physical education through gymnastics and fitness training—stretching back to Renaissance times and earlier, the Greek 5th century B.C.—its role was essentially a cultural and political one, intended to inspire nationalistic pride in the people at a time when they were struggling for independence.

Right: A family enjoys a quiet bike ride through Stromovka Park, the old royal hunting grounds in Prague.

Part of the Sokol tradition involved rallies at which thousands of people would exercise in formation in a stadium, using banners and ribbons to make striking displays. Sokol members were targeted for abuse by the Nazis during the German occupation of Czechoslovakia in World War II and by the communists after the war, but Czechs held on to the robust tradition, fulfilling Miroslav Tyrs's vision of promoting nationalism. Sokol was revived publicly after 1989. The movement spread abroad, including units in the United States and Canada. The most recent Sokol rallies were held in 2000 and 2006.

SPORTS

Czechs have endless enthusiasm for many modern sports. Soccer is a national passion, and the country is often represented in the European soccer championship matches. Czechs also enjoy a national soccer competition. Young fans admire their favorite soccer heroes and collect photos of them.

Second to soccer as a national sport is ice hockey. Czechs have participated in European and world championships since the end of the 19th century. The Czech national men's ice hockey team is one of the most successful

Czech youths vigorously pursue a game of ice hockey on a frozen pond.

In the late summer and early fall many townspeople spend weekends at their country cottages picking mushrooms. Some people concentrate on only one or two species, while others may collect dozens of different fungi. There are many ways to preserve them, and much time is spent in kitchens drying, pickling, and freezing the collected mushrooms for later use.

national teams in the world. They have won multiple World Championships and the 1998 Winter Olympic Games Hockey Champion.

Ice skating is also a favorite pastime. During the winter, when temperatures fall below freezing, sections of some parks are sprayed with water, converting them into ice rinks. Czechs also like to ski, and given the mountainous terrain of the country, there is a wide choice of slopes.

A family sits outside their Cernnosice holiday home.

Tennis has an enthusiastic following, too. The Škoda Czech Open is held in early August in Prague. Famous Czech tennis players include Martina Navrátilová and Ivan Lendl. Both of those great players are now United States citizens.

Another favorite pastime is cycling in the countryside. The Czech landscape provides many varied and stunning locations, from the foothills of mountain ranges to the lakes in South Bohemia. Not many people cycle in the larger cities because of the predominance of cobbled streets, heavy traffic, and air pollution.

A COUNTRY RETREAT

On the weekends, many Czech families head for their country cottages. The notion of a country retreat is a long-standing feature of Czech culture. These second homes may be heirloom cottages passed down through the family, cottages left vacant by people who moved to the cities, or newly built chalets on the edge of villages. Some cozy cabins are also available for short-term rentals.

After World War II, some 3 million Germans were forced to leave the Czech lands and return to Germany, abandoning their property. Czechs moved into the empty homes and possessed them by the simple process of occupying the buildings. During the communist years, when citizens were forbidden to express thoughts or beliefs contrary to the approved government policy, they would retreat to their second homes for some respite and honest conversation.

During the communist era country cottages were often in a state of extreme neglect and disrepair. More recently, people have begun to spend money renovating and restoring such properties. Czechs proudly refer to their "golden hands," noting that they are naturally adept at completing any manual task. Many happily spend the workweek planning what tasks they will tackle on the weekend, and assembling the right tools and materials.

The 1997 and 2000 floods devastated many country homes. It took time to repair the damages, but the country cottage has continued as a treasured Czech tradition.

Since Karlovy Vary was founded by Charles IV in the 14th century, many famous people have "taken the waters" at the spa towns in the Czech lands. Among them were German poet and dramatist Johann Wolfgang von Goethe, composer Johann Sebastian Bach, and socialist philosopher Karl Marx.

FREE TO TRAVEL

Recently, Czechs have become great travelers abroad. During the four decades under the communist regime, travel was not widely allowed, particularly to the West. Once the restrictions were lifted, foreign excursions became desired and realized vacations.

The most popular destination for many Czech holidaymakers has been the Croatian coast because of its sunny weather and good connections to and from the Czech Republic. Czech travelers often take extreme measures to save money and be self-sufficient. Many prefer to travel on a budget by taking their own food and supplies, including such Czech staples as sausages, beer, bread, canned meat, and dumpling mix. That makes them unpopular visitors in other countries, as they do not spend as much money as other tourists!

A recent Croatian ban on bringing in certain foods, including meat and dairy products from all EU countries, had provoked almost 90,000 angry Czechs to cancel their summer holidays there. Instead, many headed for the Adriatic coast in Italy. Some went to Spain and France, which are also becoming popular destinations for the Czechs. After much outrage, the ban was lifted in July 2008.

HEALING WATERS

A resort in the beautiful spa town of Karlovy Vary, whose springs were discovered by Charles IV.

The republic has many naturally occurring mineral springs, particularly in West Bohemia and North Moravia. Spa towns have developed where people go to treat medical conditions, usually by bathing in the mineral-infused waters or drinking it. West Bohemia spa towns include Karlovy Vary, Jáchymov, Františkovy Lázně, and Mariánské Lázně; in North Moravia a number of spa towns are located near the Jeseníky Mountains.

The spas specialize in treating one or more ailments—respiratory, thyroid, coronary, and rheumatic diseases; allergies; diseases of the liver, kidney, stomach, and skin; and gynecological complaints are some of them. Elderly Czechs in particular enjoy taking the baths, whether to treat specific ailments or simply to relax in the thermal waters. Most spa towns are surrounded by magnificent countryside.

PARKS AND THE ARTS

Larger towns and cities usually have one or more public parks, and some feature formal gardens with carefully trimmed shrubs bordering arcaded walks. Czechs of all ages take advantage of these stretches of green for strolls, picnics, or a leisurely read under the fragrant magnolia trees. In summer, the parks are filled with people throwing Frisbees, playing guitars, walking their dogs, or quietly people watching.

A favorite leisure pursuit for older Czechs is the theater, especially opera. The arts have remained a constant factor in the lives of all Czechs. Those who have the time like to attend the many festivals and concerts offered in large cities. The concerts are not as inexpensive as they once were (under the communist regime, ticket prices were subsidized), but retired citizens are still entitled to lower ticket prices.

FESTIVALS

A man in folk dress rides on a decorated horse during the Ride of Kings festival in Moravian Slovacko village.

CHAPTER 12

CZECH FESTIVALS ARE A GLORIOUS mixture of Christian and pre-Christian rituals. Throughout the country, rites celebrating the seasons are held, varying in detail according to the region. Added to those are festivals of cultural and patriotic significance to Czechs.

CHRISTIAN TRADITIONS

Under the communist regime, although the holy days of Easter and Christmas were work holidays, their religious significance was downplayed by the government.

EASTER The religious celebrations of Easter are integrated with pre-Christian rituals marking the change of seasons. The Sunday before Easter, Palm Sunday, is also a celebration of the arrival of spring. The figure of Death, made from sticks and cloth, is ceremoniously burned, representing the end of winter. Traditional Czechs decorate green branches with bright ribbons and eggs—symbolizing the cycle of new life—and bathe in springs believed to have a rejuvenating effect. In another Easter custom, beautifully decorated eggs are given away and also placed in house and shop windows. People also put other symbols of new life in their windows, such as pussy willow branches and dolls made of straw.

Many of the festivals are celebrated in both cities and rural areas, while some are unique to certain locations. For some Czechs, a name day (the day of the saint after whom one is named) is almost as important as a birthday. Calendar companies publish lists of saints' days, and these help people to remember friends' name days with small gifts or cards.

Beautifully decorated Easter eggs for sale in celebration of Easter.

One spring ritual connected with Easter persists throughout the countryside: men and boys go around gently swatting women and girls with willow switches. In some places, they also pour buckets of water on women. These gestures are meant to represent fertility and seasonal rejuvenation, and they involve much merriment.

CHRISTMAS is a time for gifts, family, fun, and feasting, as it is elsewhere. Although its religious significance has dimmed considerably, the joyful rituals and delicious cookies and other foods associated with Christmas continue to be enjoyed by many Czechs.

On Saint Nicholas's Day, December 6, Saint Nicholas and the devil together visit the homes of family and close friends. (They are usually someone's father and uncle dressed up.) Saint Nicholas looks remarkably like the Roman Catholic pope in a tall white hat and long white coat, and he carries a shepherd's staff. The devil wears a mask or heavy black makeup, horns on his head, an old fur coat, and sometimes a tail and a chain that rattles

The Christmas market in the Czech Republic attracts many to browse the stalls, listen to carols, and sip hot wine.

as he walks. Children who have been good receive a small gift such as fruit, nuts, or chocolate, whereas children who have been naughty are given a piece of coal.

Christmas Eve is also called Generous Day, and is special for its gift giving and traditional family meals. Dinner begins with carp soup, followed by carp either fried with breadcrumbs and served with potato salad, or served with black sauce. Dessert is a light fruitcake. Presents are opened with much enthusiasm after dinner. Some Czechs still like to go to midnight Mass.

Christmas Day is a family event. Lunch is traditionally roast turkey, dumplings, and sauerkraut. Adults may lift a glass or two of local wines or homemade brandies. The next day, Saint Stephen's Day, is spent recuperating. The Christmas season ends on January 6, the Day of the Three Kings, which is sometimes marked by carols and bell ringing.

COMMEMORATIVE DATES

January 19	*Anniversary of the death of Jan Palach, the Charles University student who immolated himself in 1969 in protest against the Soviet occupation of his country. Czechs offer flowers in Wenceslas Square to mark this day.*
March 7	*Birthday of Tomáš Garrigue Masaryk, Czechoslovakia's much revered first president.*
May 5	*České povstání, the anniversary of the anti-Nazi uprising by the people of Prague. The fierce fighting began on May 5, 1945, and lasted four days.*
July 3	*A mock battle commemorates the decisive Battle of Chlum on July 3, 1866, when 221,000 Prussians defeated 215,000 Austrian and Saxon troops, leaving 53,000 dead, only 9,000 of whom were Prussian. Over 460 graves and tombstones mark the battlefield. Every July, memorials are held in this little North Bohemian town. Chlum was made a commemorative zone in 1996.*

BURNING OF THE WITCHES

This broom-burning festival, celebrated on April 30, represents a pre-Christian ritual to ward off evil forces. Witches (or those suspected of being witches) in particular were targeted, for they were believed to ride off on broomsticks to rendezvous with the devil.

Today the witches' occasion is used to mark the end of winter and involves nighttime parties gathered around bonfires. There are also romantic customs for young couples—they jump over the dying embers together, and the next day the men lay branches with new leaves on the doorstep of their favorite girl.

In the Burning of the Witches ceremony, country people tidy their properties and gather on the highest hill for a ceremonial burning of their brooms as a defense against the evil witches.

STRÁŽNICE INTERNATIONAL FOLKLORE FESTIVAL

Since it was first held in 1945, the International Folklore Festival in Strážnice, Moravia, has played a key role in the preservation of traditional dress, music,

NATIONAL HOLIDAYS

January 1	*Nový rok, New Year's Day, is also the anniversary of the independence of the Czech Republic in 1993.*
March or April	*Velikonoční pondělí, Easter Monday.*
May 1	*Svátek práce, Labor Day, was very significant under the communist regime; it is now a day of enjoyment, usually spent picnicking in the countryside and often preceded by all-night revels.*
May 8	*V-E Day, Victory in Europe Day, anniversary of the end of World War II in Europe in 1945.*
July 5	*Den Cyrila a Metoděje, the saints' day for the monks Cyril and Methodius, celebrates the introduction of Christianity to Slavs and the beginning of their written language.*
July 6	*Den Jana Husa, Jan Hus Day, commemorates the burning at the stake in 1415 of the great theologian and religious reformer.*
September 28	*Den České státnosti, Czech Statehood Day*
October 28	*Den vzniku Československa, Independence Day, the anniversary of the founding of the First Czechoslovak Republic in 1918.*
November 17	*Den boje za svobodu a demokracii, Struggle for Freedom and Democracy Day. Known also as International Students' Day or the "day of students' fight for freedom and democracy," it is the anniversary of the closure of Czech universities by the Germans in 1939; it also commemorates the student demonstrations that led to the collapse of the communist government in 1989.*
December 24	*Štědrý den, Christmas Eve*
December 25	*Vánoce, Christmas Day.*
December 26	*Den sv. Štěpána, Saint Stephen's Day*

Girls in traditional dress walk in a procession during the Ride of the Kings festival.

and dance. Beloved national customs managed to survive during the years of cheerless communist rule even without official subsidies.

The festivities take place over two days in the park of a castle, with both organized and impromptu open-air musical performances, food stalls, and plenty of beer and wine. Festival highlights include a procession of costumed celebrants from all over Europe, which starts at the town's main square and makes it way to the castle park. Festivities continue into the night. Children and adults alike enjoy the occasion.

RIDE OF THE KINGS

On the last weekend of May, a few remaining towns in southeast Moravia continue the tradition of the Ride of the Kings. The festival celebrates the spring's new crops, and the ride itself relates to a young man's rite of passage, believed to harken back to an older European festival. Celebrating spring and new growth involves a lot of feasting accompanied by music and dancing. Intricately decorated folk dress is worn as part of the singing and dancing events.

For two days, the "king" recruits his court attendants, and then on Sunday they ride on horseback around town together to be accepted by the adult men. The king must be chaste, so he is usually about 12 years old. His helpers, however, may be up to 18 years old.

The king holds a rose clenched between his teeth throughout the ceremony as he is not permitted to smile. He and his courtiers are dressed

CULTURAL EVENTS

Late April—early May	*Brno International Trade Fair; Šumperk Jazz Festival*
Early May	*Czech-Moravian soccer cup final*
Mid-May	*Prague International Book Fair; Olomouc Flower Festival*
Late May	*Vlčnov Folk Festival; Prague Puppet Festival; Janáček Hukvaldy, International Music Festival*
May 12—June 4	*Pražské Jaro, Prague Spring International Music Festival*
July	*Karlovy Vary Film Festival*
Late August	*Brno International Grand Prix, motorcycling event*
Early September	*Hop and Beer Festival*
September	*Prague Mozart Festival*
Late September	*Brno International Music Festival; Teplice Beethoven Music Festival*
October	*Plzeň Beer Festival*

FESTIVALS

April 30	*Pálení Čarodějnic, Burning of the Witches*
May	*Ride of the Kings*
June	*International Folklore Festival, Strážnice*
December 6	*Saint Nicholas's Day*

in women's clothing, which is a feature of an ancient ritual to protect the crops. The horses are decorated with ribbons and paper flowers. The ceremonial ride begins at the home of the king and winds its way through the village. Along the way, the helpers call out in verse, asking for gifts for the king, and onlookers respond by placing money in the helpers' boots. The celebrations end with a parade and more singing and dancing.

Fall is a time of local festivals associated with the harvest. On such occasions, a pig may be roasted to celebrate the year's gifts of crops and vintage.

FOOD

Peppers for sale at the Havelske market in Stare Mesto, Prague.

CHAPTER 13

OVER THE CENTURIES CZECH CUISINE has absorbed Austrian, Hungarian, German, and Polish influences. The traditional Hungarian goulash and German sauerkraut have become Czech staples. Czechs enjoy the Slavic custom of flavoring foods with sour cream, lemon, vinegar, and green grapes.

Fresh produce is not a large part of the Czech diet due to the cold Czech environment. The seafood that is available is largely fish that have been raised in artificial lakes or fish farms.

TRADITIONAL FARE

A typical Czech meal includes lots of meat and large portions of dumplings, potatoes, or rice covered in a thick sauce, accompanied by vegetables or sauerkraut. For their meat dish, Czechs prefer pork but like other meats, too. Poultry is roasted, whether chicken or the favorite—farm-bred goose. A roast beef is served with the ever present dumplings and sauerkraut.

Czechs also enjoy preserved or pickled vegetables. Fresh vegetables, with the exception of salads, are not a regular dish in a Czech menu. Bacon, caraway seeds, and salt are typical flavorings. In the fall Czechs greatly enjoy the bountiful supply of a variety of mushrooms, which they pick on trips to the countryside.

Right: A fruit stall in a colorful open-air market.

As the republic is landlocked, seafood is generally not present on the dining table. Trout fished from mountain streams, however, is enjoyed by Czechs, as is carp from the ancient artificial ponds in South Bohemia. A feast with carp as the main dish is the traditional fare for Christmas Eve.

Bread is made in many styles, although rye bread is by far the most common, often flavored with caraway seeds.

Favorite snacks are smoked meats, cheese, or thick, spicy pork or beef sausages, which may be fried or boiled. The sausages are often served with mustard. Rye and wheat bread will often be served with cold meats and cheeses. Patties made from grated raw potato and garlic are also a typical fast-food snack.

Breakfast at home typically consists of bread with butter, jam, or yogurt; cheese; eggs; ham or sausage; and tea or coffee. Workers rushing off to work may stop at a small café, often equipped with a narrow counter or small, tall tables, which they stand around to quickly consume soup, rolls, and sausages. Some Czechs take sandwiches to work to eat during their 10 A.M. break. Lunch is the main meal, but is usually a hurried affair, except on Sundays. When people can afford it, they go out for lunch and are always happy to enjoy a long break. Dinner will be a light meal and may consist of a cold buffet of meats and cheese with bread.

A vendor fishes carp out for sale from a tub. A feast with carp has been a long-standing Czech Christmas tradition.

The kitchen is still very much a woman's domain. Many women prefer that their husbands stay out of the kitchen altogether and think nothing of spending several hours preparing the main meal without help. For a husband to wash the dishes is a very offbeat occurrence in most households.

A typical Sunday lunch usually begins with soup. It may be a light broth with savory pieces of bacon, vegetables, or noodles; or a thick and heavy soup, such as potato with vegetables and mushrooms; sliced tripe in broth with spices; or a thick and spicy beef and potato soup. The main course often consists of dumplings, sauerkraut, and roasted pork chops or goose. Other very common selections are roast beef and goulash, served with a dill cream sauce or mushroom sauce. A Czech specialty is roast beef served with lemon, cranberries, and bread dumplings in a sour cream sauce. French fries or rice may accompany the main course. Local beer, rather than imported soft drinks, usually accompanies every course of a meal.

Sauerkraut is a popular side dish that accompanies many Czech meals.

DUMPLINGS AND DESSERTS

Dumplings are a common part of Czech cuisine. They are served with most main courses and are also made in sweet versions for dessert. Typical savory (meaning not sweet) dumplings are made with either a bread or potato base. *Kynute knedlíky* (KNED-liki, raised dumplings), which is made from milk, eggs, and yeast, rises like bread. A traditional dish at Christmas lunch is bread or liver dumplings, the latter flavored with lemon zest and marjoram. A favorite sweet dessert is plum dumpling, where dried plums (prunes) are wrapped in a thin layer of dough, boiled, and then rolled in crushed poppy seeds mixed with cinnamon sugar. Fruit dumplings are a summer specialty, made not only with plums but also with blueberries and apricots, dripping with melted butter and served with cottage cheese.

Another favorite dessert with adults and children alike is *vanilkové rohlíčky*. This crescent-shaped cookie, flavored with vanilla, lemon, and almonds or walnuts and dusted with confectioners' sugar, is served especially during Christmas.

WHAT TO DRINK

A Czech usually offers a guest strong, sweet "Turkish-style" coffee. Hot water is poured over finely ground beans that end up as a paste at the bottom of the cup. Tea, which is not as popular as coffee, is commonly served with lemon. On a hot day, beer is offered. Few Czechs drink tap water. This reluctance was

A mature vineyard at Ratiskovice.

reinforced after the floods of 1997 and 2000, which contaminated many drinking water supplies.

Although Czechs are great beer consumers, Moravia is well known as a wine-growing region, especially in the southeast. A favorite pastime for friends and family is to gather at family-run wine cellars to taste wine and sing. A drink widely enjoyed in summer is white wine and soda water on ice. This seasonal mix is known in America as a spritzer. Czechs prefer hot wine in the winter.

Moravia is also famous for its fiery brandies, both plum and apricot, as well as cherry liqueurs. A popular drink all year-round is a mixture of rum and hot water in equal parts, flavored with lemon. The spa town of Karlovy Vary jealously guards the recipe to its locally produced spicy herbal liqueur, Becherovka, which is often served as an aperitif.

FAMOUS BEERS Beer drinkers have a choice of a great variety of good beers, especially in Prague, for the home of Czech beer is Bohemia. The earliest record of the brewing tradition in Prague is a document dated 1082, while the famous brewing town of Plzeň (Pilsen) was allowed to produce its own beer in 1290. Czechs drink 34 gallons (129 l) per capita each year—equivalent to more than 300 pint glasses of beer. Czechs drink the greatest amount of beer in the world per capita. The Czech Republic was the first country to have a beer museum as well as the first beer-brewing textbook.

After a serious operation and many days in intensive care, vanilla crescents were the first food asked for by the first president of the Czech Republic, Václav Havel.

In Bohemia beer accompanies most meals, including breakfast. Czechs drink beer the way Americans drink soft drinks. Beer is served almost everywhere except in wine bars. Most Czech beers are lagers, naturally brewed from handpicked hops—the catkins of the hop vine—and contain between 3 percent and 6 percent alcohol. People like to drink their beer cold with a creamy head. Beer is known as *pivo* in all Slavonic languages.

Premium Czech beers such as Budvar and Pilsener Urquell are well-known throughout the world. Budvar, the original Budweiser beer, is exported to 21 countries. One of Bohemia's oldest beers is the brand Regent, which has been in production since 1379. Bohemian beers are believed to be the best in the world because of the superior quality of Bohemian hops.

The Plzensky Prazdroj Brewery, where Pilsner Urquell Beer is brewed.

EATING OUT

Czech towns and cities have many different types of eating places, with the widest range of cuisines found in Prague. Czechs love to eat out and do so whenever their budget allows. A visiting friend is reason enough to have dinner at a popular restaurant or to step out for a beer at the pub.

In Prague alone there are more than 2,700 pubs and inns, some of which were established centuries ago. The historical pubs are now tourist haunts. Pubs serve food as well as beer, some of them running to roasts, goulash, sauerkraut—and, of course, dumplings. Wine bars usually sell snacks as well, and some serve full meals. The wines found in most bars are from Czech or Slovakian wineries.

Many Czechs frequent simple, self-service, cafeteria-style places, that offer soups and staples such as dumplings, sandwiches, salads, sausages, and goulash at reasonable prices. In Prague there is a tradition of elegant coffeehouses that serve coffee as well as numerous other drinks, except beer, and a selection of snacks and pastries. Recent innovations are bookshops with cafés or restaurants attached. Slovak-style rustic restaurants, which are found throughout the Czech Republic, typically serve barbecued chicken. Vegetarians have limited choices when dining out.

Eating and drinking are significant activities for Czechs, and the portions served in restaurants are generous. For good food and a convivial atmosphere, there is no better place to sample the traditional fare of the republic than in one of its numerous bars, cafés, or restaurants.

VEPČOVÁ PEČENĚ (ROAST PORK)

6–8 servings

4–6 (2–3 kg) pounds pork butt or shoulder

2 tablespoons (30 ml) caraway seeds

1 tablespoon (15 ml) salt

2 teaspoons (10 ml) pepper

2 tablespoons (30 ml) cooking oil

3 onions, coarsely chopped

2 carrots, coarsely chopped

½ cup water (125 ml), stock, white wine, or beer

2–3 tablespoons (30–45 ml) flour

2–3 tablespoons (30–45 ml) butter

Mix caraway, salt, pepper, and oil in a small bowl. Rub pork all over with spice mixture, then marinate for at least an hour, preferably overnight. Bring meat to room temperature. Preheat oven to 350°F (180°C). Mix chopped onions and carrots and place in a roasting pan. Pour the water, stock, white wine, or beer into the pan. Place roast, fat side down, on top of vegetables. Cover pan with foil, and roast for an hour.

Remove foil from the pan and turn roast fat side up. Cut deep crosshatches in the fat in a diamond pattern, then place the roast, uncovered, back in the oven. Roast for another 1 ½ to 2 hours, or until the roast is tender and well browned. A meat thermometer inserted into the center of the roast should read 165°F (74°C). Remove the roast to a cutting board, cover it lightly with foil and let it rest for about 20 minutes.

Make the gravy by kneading the flour and butter together with your fingers to make a doughy paste and set aside. Strain the pan juices from the roasting pan. Add enough water, stock, wine, or beer to the pan juices to make 2 cups (500 ml). Bring the pan juices to a simmer in a saucepan over medium heat. Whisk small pieces of the butter-flour paste into the pan juices until the gravy is thickened. Reduce heat to low and simmer for 5 to 10 minutes. Season to taste. Carve the roast in thin slices and serve with the gravy on the side.

PLUM CAKE

2 cups (500 ml) flour

¼ teaspoon (1.25 ml) baking powder

1 ½ pounds (0.68 kg) prune plums

1 teaspoon (5 ml) cinnamon

½ teaspoon (2.5 ml) vanilla extract

½ cup (125 ml) confectioners' sugar

1 tablespoon (15 ml) lemon juice

whipped cream (optional)

Preheat the oven to 350°F (180°C).

Put ½ cup (125 ml) of granulated sugar, the vanilla extract and the lemon juice into a mixing bowl and cut in the butter. Mix together well. Break in the two eggs and beat them into the sugar mixture until light and creamy, about 5 minutes. Mix together the flour and baking powder, then gradually incorporate the flour mixture into the sugar-egg mixture.

Cut the plums in half and remove their pits. Put the plum halves into a bowl, add the remaining ½ cup of sugar (125 ml) and the cinnamon, and mix well.

Butter a 9" by 13" (23 cm by 33 cm) round baking pan and then fill it evenly with the batter. Space the plum halves, cut side up, all over the cake. Place in the preheated oven and bake until done, about 30 minutes. Sprinkle with the confectioners' sugar. Serve with whipped cream if desired.

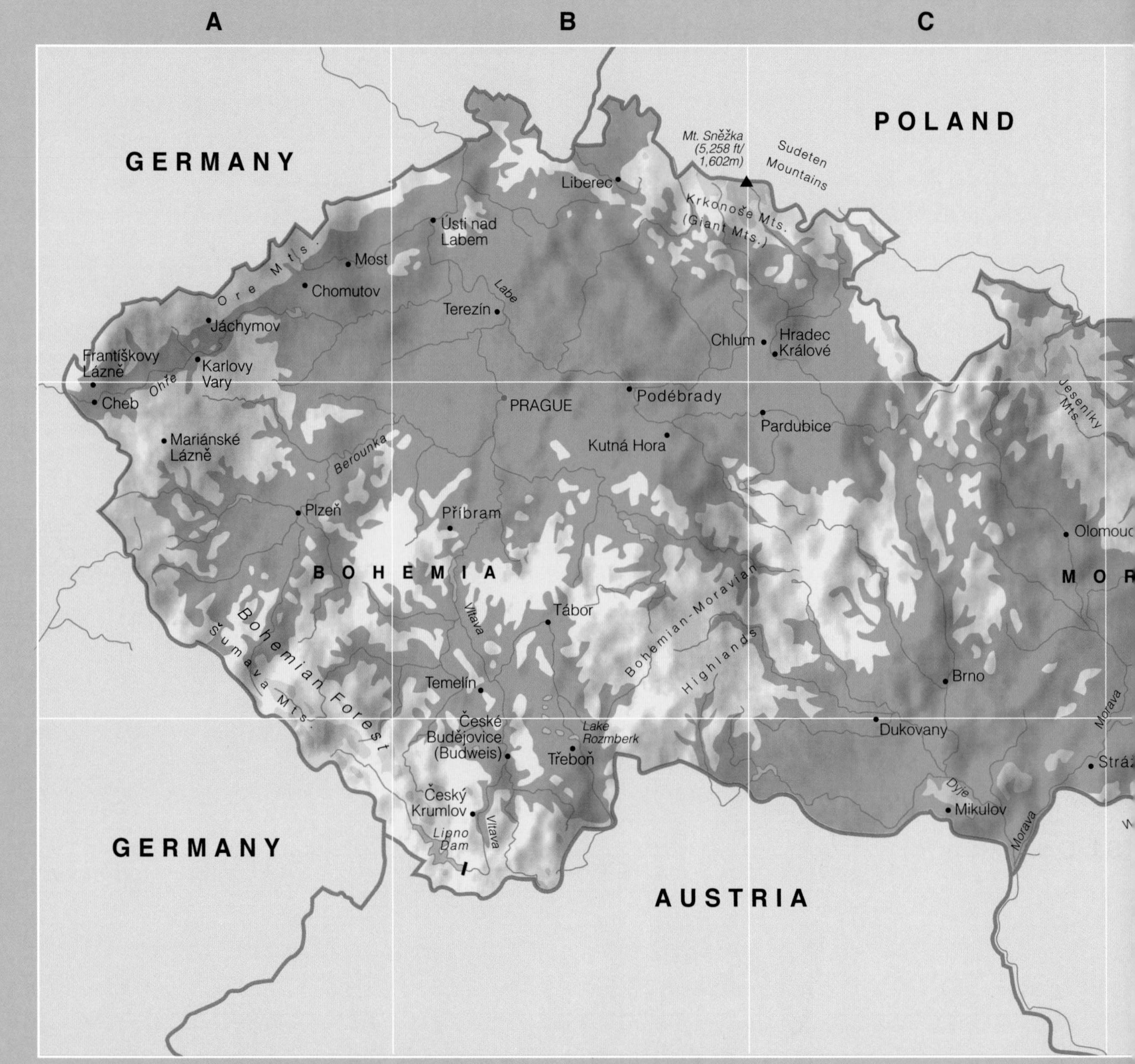
A
B
C
1
2
3
GERMANY
POLAND
Mt. Sněžka (5,258 ft/ 1,602m)
Sudeten Mountains
Liberec
Krkonoše Mts. (Giant Mts.)
Ústi nad Labem
Most
Ore Mts.
Chomutov
Labe
Terezín
Jáchymov
Chlum
Hradec Králové
Františkovy Lázně
Karlovy Vary
Ohře
Cheb
Poděbrady
PRAGUE
Pardubice
Jeseníky Mts.
Mariánské Lázně
Kutná Hora
Berounka
Plzeň
Příbram
Olomouc
BOHEMIA
MOR
Bohemian-Moravian Highlands
Tábor
Vltava
Bohemian Forest
Šumava Mts.
Temelín
Brno
Morava
České Budějovice (Budweis)
Lake Rozmberk
Třeboň
Dukovany
Dyje
Mikulov
Český Krumlov
Lipno Dam
Vltava
GERMANY
AUSTRIA
Morava

MAP OF THE CZECH REPUBLIC

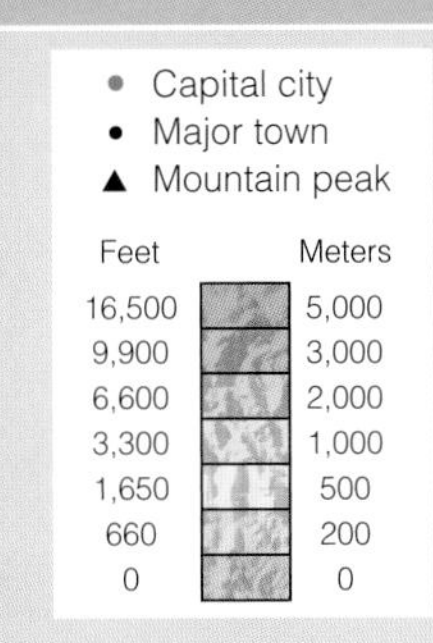

Austria, A3, B3, C3

Berounka, A2
Bohemia, A2, B2
Bohemia-Moravian Highlands, B2, C2
Bohemian Forest, A2–3
Brno, C2

Cheb, A2
Chlum, C1
Chomutov, A1

Dukovany, C2–3
Dyje (river), C3

Františkovy Lázně, A2

Germany, A1–3, B1

Hradec Králové, C1

Jáchymov, A1
Javorniky Mountains, D2
Jeseniky Mountains, C2

Karlovy Vary, A1
Kroknoše Mountain, B1, C1
Kutná Hora, B2

Labe (river), B1
Liberec, B1

Mariánské Lázně, A2
Mikulov, C3
Morava (river), D2, C3
Moravia, C2, D2
Most, A1

Odra, D2
Ohře, A1–2
Olomouc, C2
Ore Mountains, A1–A2, B2
Ostrava, D2

Pardubice, C2
Plzeň, A2
Podèbrady, B2
Poland, B1, C1, D1–2
Prague, B2
Příbram, B2

Silesia, D2
Slovakia, C3, D3
Sněžka Mountain, B1, C1
Strážnice, C3
Šumava Mountains, A2

Temelin, B2

Usti nad Labem, B1

Vltava (river), B2–3

White Carpathian Mountains, D3

Zlin, D2

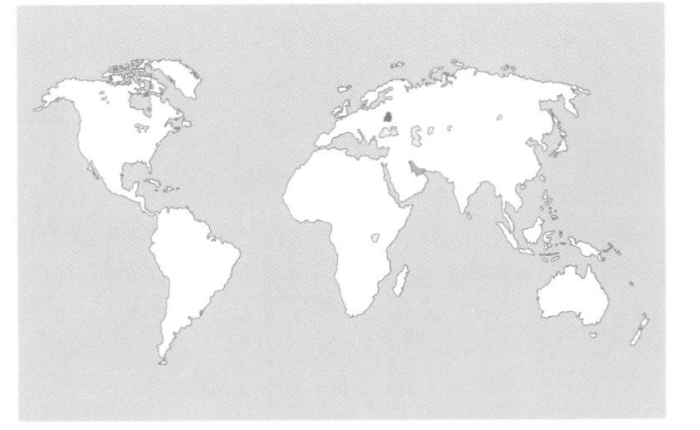

ECONOMIC CZECH REPUBLIC

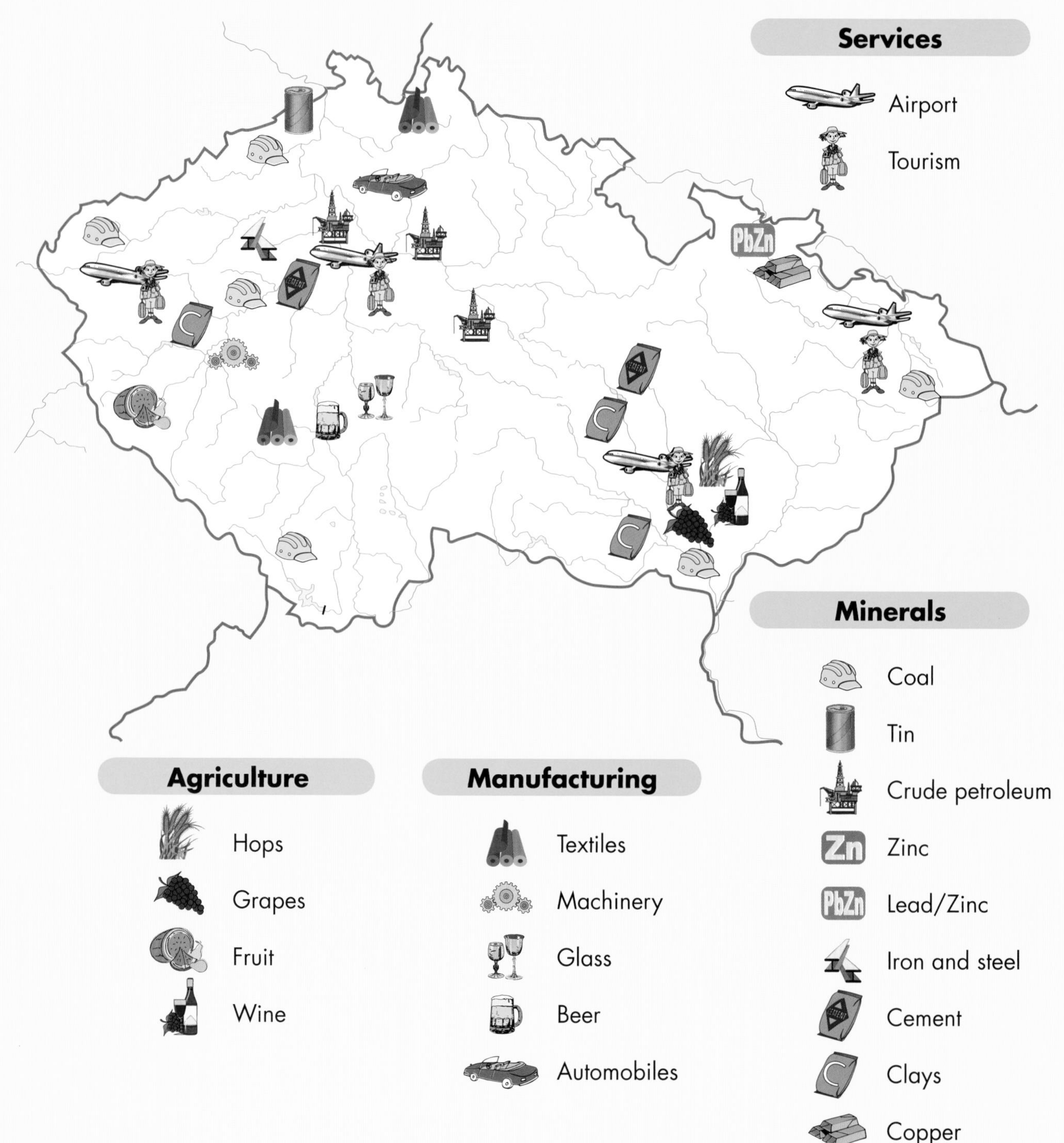

ABOUT THE ECONOMY

OVERVIEW

The Czech Republic has one of the more successful economies of all the former communist Eastern European countries. It suffered some setbacks in the late 1990s when the country was hit with both an economic crisis and a political scandal. During the 1990s there was a significant amount of Western investment. It has been a member of NATO since 1990 and a member of the EU since 2004. It performs strongly in the areas of industry and services. Its main industrial products include iron and steel, machinery and equipment, motor vehicles, chemicals, armaments, textiles, glass, and ceramics. Its service sector does particularly well in areas of finance and insurance.

GROSS DOMESTIC PRODUCT (GDP)

$248.9 billion (2007 estimate)

GDP PER CAPITA

$24,200 (2007 estimate)

GROWTH RATE

6.5 percent (2007 estimate)

CURRENCY

Czech koruna (Kč or, internationally, CZK)
USD1.00 = 19.16 CZK (January 2009 estimate)

MAIN EXPORTS

Agricultural products (wheat, potatoes, sugar beets, hops, fruits), textiles, vehicles (the Škoda car), machinery and transport equipment, chemicals, raw materials and fuels, electric equipment and electronics, iron and steel, ceramics, glass, beers, and armaments.

MAIN IMPORTS

Machinery, electric equipment and electronics, mineral fuels and oils, vehicles, and plastics.

LABOR FORCE

5.36 million (2007 estimate)

TOURISM

6.68 million visitors (2007 estimate)
Revenue: $5.68 billion.(2006 estimate)

MAIN TRADE PARTNERS

Germany, Slovakia, Poland, Hungary, Russia, Switzerland, Bulgaria, and other former USSR republics.

AGRICULTURAL PRODUCTS

Wheat, potatoes, sugar beets, hops, fruits

NATURAL RESOURCES

Hard coal, soft coal, lignite (brown coal), kaolin (clay), graphite, coke, timber, uranium, magnesite

CULTURAL CZECH REPUBLIC

Plzen (or Pilsen)
Plzen is world renowned for its locally brewed beer—Pilsner Urquell. Built in the 13th century, the elegant town is an example of high-Gothic urbanism. The medieval Cathedral of Saint Bartholomew there claims the highest church tower in Bohemia.

Karlovy Vary (or Karlsbad)
Established around 1350, the famous Karlovy Vary spa is the largest spa in the Czech Republic. It was built by the Holy Roman Emperor and Czech king Charles IV.

Prague Castle
Along with Charles Bridge and Josefov (the Jewish quarter), Prague Castle is one of the city's main attractions. Since 1918 the venerable fortress has been the official seat of the president of the republic. Prague Castle was founded in the late ninth century.

Trebon
Established in the 12th century, Trebon is popular as a small spa town and is also a center of fish farming. Its Renaissance chateau is connected to the Rožmberk library and the Augustinian Monastery. The tomb of the Schwarzenbergs, the last aristocratic family in Trebon, is another interesting sight.

The Old Jewish Cemetery, Prague
The Old Jewish Cemetery and Old-New Synagogue date back to the beginning of the 15th century. Burials took place at the cemetery until 1787. Today, approximately 12,000 gravestones stand in place, which include tombs of the primate of Prague's Jewish district, Mordecai Markus Maisel (died 1601), and historian and astronomer David Gans (died 1613).

Villa Tugendhat, Brno
The Villa Tugendhat, a UNESC World Heritage site, is the very firs monument of modern architecture i the Czech Republic. Named after Frit Tugendhat, owner of a Brno textil factory, this landmark glass-fronte villa was designed by the famou German architect Ludwig Mies va der Rohe in 1928.

Ceský Krumlov
This castle city in the southwest of the Czech Republic has preserved its medieval center. Since 1992 it has been a UNESCO World Heritage site and one of the republic's most visited places. The castle of Ceský Krumlov, with its distinctive red gate, is the second-biggest castle in Bohemia, incorporating over 40 buildings, 5 courtyards, and numerous parks. It took more than six centuries to complete the castle.

Ceský Krumlov (or Krumau)
Ceský Krumlov, also a UNESCO site, is a unique historical town with a famous castle complex, one of the largest in Central Europe. It also has a beautiful Baroque theater and a well-preserved historical center from the Middle Ages.

Telc
Telc is a small town, probably established in the 13th century. It has the honor of being included on the UNESCO Cultural Heritage List. Its historical central space, Nám stí Zachariáše z Hradce, is one of the most beautiful triangular "squares" in the republic.

Lednice
The village of Lednice is a UNESCO World Heritage site. It contains a palace and the largest park in the country, covering an area of approximately 77 square miles (200 square km). The palace started its career as a Renaissance villa; in the 17th century it became a summer residence of the ruling princes of Liechtenstein.

ABOUT THE CULTURE

OFFICIAL NAME
Czech Republic

CAPITAL
Prague

AREA
30,450 square miles (78,866 square km)

POPULATION
10,220,900 (July 2008 estimate)

PROVINCES
One capital city and 13 regions or administrative divisions—hlavní město Praha (capital city Prague), Středočeský kraj (Central Bohemia), Jihočeský kraj (South Bohemia), Plzečský kraj (Pilsen), Karlovarský kraj, Ústecký kraj, Liberecký kraj, Královéhradecký kraj, Pardubický kraj, Vysočina, Jihomoravský kraj, Olomoucký kraj, Zlínský kraj, Moravskoslezský kraj

MAJOR CITIES
Prague, Brno, Ostrava, Plzeň, Olomouc, Liberec

MAJOR RIVERS
Labe (Elbe), Vltava (Moldau), Ohře, Odra (Oder), Morava, Lužnice, Jihlava, and Svratka rivers

OFFICIAL LANGUAGE
Czech

ETHNIC GROUPS
Czech 90.4 percent, Moravian 3.7 percent, Slovak 1.9 percent, other 4 percent (2001 census)

MAJOR RELIGIONS
Roman Catholic 26.8 percent, Protestant 2.1 percent, other 3.3 percent, unspecified 8.8 percent, unaffiliated 59 percent (2001 census)

BIRTHRATE
8.89 births per 1,000 population
(2008 estimate)

DEATH RATE
10.69 deaths per 1,000 population
(2008 estimate)

INFANT MORTALITY RATE
3.83 deaths per 1,000 live births

FERTILITY RATE
1.23 children born per woman

LIFE EXPECTANCY
Total population: 76.62 years
Male: 73.34 years
Female: 80.08 years (2008 estimates)

TIME LINE

IN BELARUS	IN THE WORLD
550 Slavs begin settling in the eastern Alps.	**323 B.C.** Alexander the Great's empire stretches from Greece to India.
1085 Vratislav II becomes the first king of the Czech Přemysl dynasty.	
	1206–1368 Genghis Khan unifies the Mongols and starts conquest of the world. At its height, the Mongol Empire under Kublai Khan stretches from China to Persia and parts of Europe and Russia.
1306 The Přemysl dynasty ends with the death of King Wenceslas III.	
1420–34 The Hussite Wars.	
1526–1790 The Hapsburg dynasty ascends.	
	1776 U.S. Declaration of Independence
	1789–99 The French Revolution
1848 The Czechs convene the first Slavic Congress.	
	1861 The U.S. Civil War begins.
	1914 World War I begins.
1918 Czech lands and Slovakia consolidate, establishing the independent nation of Czechoslovakia.	
1939 Czechoslovakia invaded by Hitler's army.	**1939** World War II begins.
1945 Prague Uprising; the territories of the Czech Republic liberated.	**1945** The United States drops atomic bombs on Hiroshima and Nagasaki. World War II ends.
1968 Five Warsaw Pact member countries invade Czechoslovakia; Soviet troops continue to occupy the country until 1989.	
1945–89 Communist era, dominated by Soviet Union.	
	1986 Nuclear power disaster at Chernobyl in Ukraine

IN CZECH REPUBLIC	IN THE WORLD
1989 Velvet Revolution brings an end to communism in the country.	
1993 Czech Republic gains independence when Czechoslovakia splits into two countries.	
1997 Václav Klaus government resigns following the collapse of the coalition and amid growing dissatisfaction. Josef Tošovský steps in as prime minister of the Czech Republic in a caretaker government.	**1997** Hong Kong is returned to China.
1998 Václav Havel reelected president in January for another five-year term.	
1999 Czech Republic receives full NATO membership in March.	
	2001 Terrorists crash planes into New York, Washington D.C., and Pennsylvania.
2002 Prague and other towns and villages damaged by severe flooding. At Copenhagen summit, Czech Republic is invited to join EU.	
2003 Former prime minister Václav Klaus elected president	**2003** War in Iraq begins.
2004 Czech Republic joins the EU.	
2006 Mirek Topolánek appointed as prime minister for the second time.	
2008 Václav Klaus reelected as president; Czech Republic signs agreement permitting the United States to place some of its planned missile defense shield on Czech territory. Russia threatens to retaliate.	

GLOSSARY

Art Nouveau
Art style of the late 19th and early 20th centuries, characterized by flowing forms.

babička **(BAB-ich-ka).**
Grandmother

Bohemia
Geographical region in western Czech Republic.

Bohemian crystal
A famous type of crystal that has been cut in Bohemia for centuries.

Hapsburg (also spelled Habsburg)
Austrian-German dynasty that ruled the Czech lands from 1526 until 1914.

Hradčany
A castle and its environs in Prague.

Hussite movement/Hussites
Religious movement named after the theologian and reformer Jan Hus (1369?–1415), whose followers were called Hussites.

knedlíky **(KNED-liki)**
Sweet or savory dumplings made from either a bread or potato base.

Moravia
Geographical region in eastern Czech Republic.

National Revival Movement
Czech nationalist movement in the late 18th and early 19th centuries, which saw the flowering of Czech literature, music, theater, and language.

Pan, Paní, Slec˘na (PAHN, PA-ni, SLE-tchna)
Mister, Missus, Miss—forms of address.

Prague Spring
A period in the 1960s under President Alexander Dubček when civil liberties were greater than had been usual under the communist regime.

Přemysl dynasty (PRZHE-mysl)
A dynasty founded by and named after a peasant, Přemysl, who ruled Bohemia in the ninth century.

sauerkraut
Sweet-sour pickled cabbage, a common dish reflecting German influence.

Silesia
Historical region found in the northeastern corner of the Czech Republic, as well as in Poland and Germany.

skansen **(SKAN-suhn)**
A Swedish term for an open-air museum of traditional architecture and furnishings.

Sokol
Exercise with banners and ribbons, performed by thousands of Czechs at rallies, often political.

FOR FURTHER INFORMATION

BOOKS

Bianchi, Elena. *Czech Republic: The Crossroads of European Culture* (Countries of the World). Vercelli, Italy: White Star, April 2006.

Bultje, Jan Williem. *Looking at the Czech Republic* (Looking at Europe). Minneapolis, MN: Oliver Press, 2006.

Humphreys, Rob. *Czech Republic* (Country Insights). London: Hodder Wayland, 2006.

Nollen, Tim. *Czech Republic* (Culture Shock). Singapore: Marshall Cavendish International (Asia), 2006.

Otfinoski, Steven. *The Czech Republic* (Nations in Transition). New York: Facts on File, 2004.

Pernal, M., T. Darmochwal, M. Ruminski, J. Sito, B. Sudnik-Wojcikowska. *Czech and Slovak Republics* (Eyewitness Travel Guides). London: Dorling Kindersley, 2006.

Roux, Lindy. *Czech Republic* (Countries of the World). Chicago: Gareth Stevens, 2004.

FILMS

Dark Blue World with Charles Dance, Tara Fitzgerald, Anna Massey, Oldřich Kaiser, Ondřej Vetchý; directed by Jan Svěrák, 2002.

Czech Republic: A Musical Journey. Smetana/Dvořák, 2008.

MUSIC

God's Simple Gifts. Folklore Children Ensemble Notičky, 2005.

Along the Berounka River. Folklore Children Ensemble Notičky, 2000.

BIBLIOGRAPHY

Brooks, Stephen. *National Geographic Traveler: Prague & the Czech Republic*. Washington D.C.: National Geographic Society, 2004.

Dunford, Lisa. *Czech & Slovak Republics* (Country Guide). 5th ed. London: Lonely Planet, 2007.

Otfinoski, Steven. *The Czech Republic* (Nations in Transition). 2 ed. New York: Facts on File, July 2004.

Rosenleaf Ritter, Nicole. *Czech Republic—Culture Smart!: A Quick Guide to Customs and Etiquette*. London: Kuperard, 2006.

Steves, Rick and Vihan, Honza. *Rick Steves' Prague and the Czech Republic*. 4th ed. Emeryville, CA: Avalon Travel Publishing, 2008.

BBC Country Profile Czech Republic. http://news.bbc.co.uk/2/hi/europe/country_profiles/1108489.stm

Ceské Noviny (Czech news in English). www.ceskenoviny.cz/news

CIA World Fact Book. www.cia.gov/cia.gov/cia/publications/factbook/index.html

Czech Republic. www.czech.cz

Encyclopaedia Britannica online. www.britannica.com

Infoplease. www.infoplease.com/ipa/A0107456.html

Radio Praha.www.radio.cz/en

UNESCO. http://portal.unesco.org/science/fr/ev.php-URL_ID=5629&URL_DO=DO_TOPIC&URL_SECTION=201.html

U.S. Department of State. Background Note: Czech Republic. www.state.gov/r/pa/ei/bgn/3237.htm

U.S. Department of State. Czech Republic. www.state.gov/g/drl/rls/irf/2005/51548.htm

INDEX

INDEX

BOCA RATON PUBLIC LIBRARY, FLORIDA
3 3656 0512580 2